L.L. Bean
Upland Bird Hunting Handbook

L.L. Bean

Upland Bird Hunting Handbook

TOM HUGGLER

The Lyons Press
Guilford, Connecticut
An imprint of The Globe Pequot Press

The Lyons Press is an imprint of The Globe Pequot Press

Printed in the United States of America

10 9 8 7 6 5 4 3 2 1

Library of Congress Cataloging-in-Publication Data

Huggler, Thomas E.
    L.L. Bean upland bird hunting handbook / Tom Huggler.
        p. cm.
    ISBN 1-58574-252-X
    1. Upland game bird shooting.   I. Title: Upland bird hunting handbook.
    II. Title.
    SK323.H85 2001
    799.2'46—dc21
                                                            2001041415

Contents

Prologue

Tom Huggler with partners Boo and Sherlock in western North Dakota.

It grows more expensive every year. Finding a good covert to replace the one that turned into the Wal-Mart outlet is harder than ever. More private land is posted or leased or otherwise off-limits. Gun laws expand, seemingly in inverse ratio to shrinking bag limits.

The odds of your finding time to train the dog, get rid of that flubber gut, and get out to the sporting clays range—in six weeks or less—is about as certain as Sisyphus reaching the hilltop or losing his boulder. The prospect of squeezing a few days into your cramped schedule for a Texas quail hunt this year seems equally remote.

So, why in the world do you want to hunt birds? What's wrong with you, anyway?

Well, if you're like me, you can't help it.

For nearly 50 years I've been following dogs that follow scent vapors left by beautiful birds that live in some of the world's most fascinating places. I'm always seven years old, carrying the plump pheasant with the oilslick breast feathers and the tack-like spurs that cut into my palm. My father shot the bird the ghostly setter had pointed, and then Dad let me administer the *coup de grace* with my Red Ryder BB gun. Shards of wheat stubble found their way inside my PF Flyers. God's eyes were wondrously blue.

I hunt birds because the alternative is depressing. To me, golf is an overly competitive game played on artificial acres. Sure, bird hunting can be just as competitive, but I guess I've outgrown the need. These days I contend with no one but myself.

I hunt birds because a journey is always involved—even when it's a short stroll to see if a migrant woodcock has found the seep behind my house. I assure you I am no good if I don't go. My late friend, Carl Parker of upstate New York, got it right when he said, "By late summer I develop a nervous twitch and start looking for a cat to kick."

I hunt birds for health. My mind is more lucid and less troubled when I am walking toward a mountaintop, double gun over my shoulder. There is a kind of poetry to it all—the limitless sky, bird song coming down the wind, the smell of grass and leaves returning to earth—and I like to think my gait is loosely iambic.

My wife and I live on 27 rural acres in southern Michigan, the area where we were both born and raised. She is also a bird hunter, and we share a reverence for land and the wild things that grow there. We raise wildflowers and native prairie grasses, build bluebird boxes and bat houses, selectively harvest our mature timber, feed songbirds, and enjoy identifying them along with toads, snakes, and butterflies. We have killed deer, woodcock, rabbits, and pheasants in this area. I taught the neighbor boy how to catch muskrats and raccoons from the winding stream beyond the seep. I would shoot mourning doves if they were legal to hunt in Michigan.

Hunting allows me to be an active participant in the balance of nature. The harvesting of any natural resource—be it timber, mushrooms, fish, or game—makes me feel part of the complex web of life that surrounds me, a web that naturally involves cycles of scarcity and abundance, of life and death.

So, come with me. Although it's true that what we gain from hunting birds is as personal as the fingerprints we leave on our gun barrels, it is also a sport meant to be shared. After all, it's not *that* much fun to hunt alone.

Tom Huggler
Sunfield, Michigan
www.tomhuggler.com
July 2001

Preface
(A Note from L.L. Bean)

L.L. Bean has been a trusted name in hunting for nearly 90 years. From our original Maine Hunting Shoe®, first introduced in 1912, to our newest Gore-Tex® Upland Field Gear, we take a special pride in providing hunters with quality gear they can trust in the field.

Our founder, Leon Leonwood Bean, built the company on his Golden Rule: "Sell good merchandise at a reasonable profit, treat your customers like human beings, and they'll always come back for more." Though we've grown and developed as a company, we've stayed true to our honest, hardworking values. We continue to stand by L.L.'s Golden Rule. We believe that the customer comes first in all things, and we hope our gear reflects this.

Our outdoor heritage guides everything we do here at L.L. Bean. We are a company of outdoorspeople. We spend countless hours in the field developing and testing our gear before you ever see it in our catalogs. If our products don't hold up to our own rigorous standards, then we simply won't sell them. Our legendary guarantee reflects this commitment: We ask you to return anything that is not completely satisfactory in every way.

When you next embark on a trip into the outdoors, we hope you'll trust L.L. Bean to provide the gear that will help make your trip safe, successful, and enjoyable. We would very much like to be your guide to the world of hunting.

CHAPTER 1

Picking a Place and a Time

Every summer, usually on or about August 1, my phone starts ringing. Someone wants to know the best places to go hunting for pheasants or quail or ruffed grouse. Maybe it's a friend who has been working out, getting ready for a Western chukar hunt. He wonders what state has the best hunting, and is there a possibility of sharptails and Huns, too? Or the person could be someone with a young dog he wants to stick into a woodcock covert close to home. These callers know that I love bird hunting, and that I try to keep up on populations and gunning opportunities throughout the country.

As a writer and passionate bird hunter, I do these things for a living. There are worse jobs—I know because I have had a few. But if you were one of the callers and wanted some inside information on where to hunt birds this fall, this is the formula I would recommend.

DEVISE A REALISTIC PLAN

First, evaluate your situation. Where will you go, and how much time do you have? Will you fly or drive? Take the dog or leave him home? Does your budget allow for a guide who will have leased ground to hunt? What kind of physical condition are you (and your dog) in? Be realistic with your answers.

One evening a few years ago, a fellow I know brought three friends to my southern Michigan home to "pick my brain" for an out-of-state pheasant hunt. We spent a few hours pouring over maps and talking about the possibilities. Because they had only five days to hunt, I suggested Iowa, which they could reach in about 12 hours from our homes in southern Michigan. "Get your licenses through the mail," I advised, "so you won't be looking for a county courthouse after they've closed for the day. Go later this fall, certainly after deer hunting season, when you'll have better luck getting access to private land."

Later, the guy blamed me for what he said was "the hunt from Hell." Their first mistake was in choosing Kansas, 500 miles farther than Iowa; they spent more than half their time driving. Although they were able to buy nonresident hunting licenses over the counter, the youngster in the group had left his hunter's training certificate home and was refused the sale. Because they couldn't find absentee landowners to secure hunting permission, they settled for public land.

"You didn't tell me those public hunting areas were so huge," he complained. "We wore ourselves out by noon of the first day. What few birds we saw were on high alert, and we didn't shoot any. I never even fired my gun. My dog was so sore the next morning he could hardly move."

I felt bad for the man and his friends, even though he had engineered his own failure. Why hadn't they gotten licensed through the mail? They had

Some public hunting areas, such as the Fort Pierre National Grassland in South Dakota, are huge, offering bird hunters plenty of space to roam.

three months to get their dog and their own bodies in shape. Why didn't they? Pheasant hunting is no cakewalk, so what were they thinking? Why only one dog for four men? And why Kansas, when time was so short?

DO THE HOMEWORK

To my way of thinking, doing your homework is part of the fun of any hunting trip. You need contacts and there are several ways to get them in the area you plan to hunt. Try running a classified ad in the local newspaper and offer to swap a hunting or fishing trip with a local sportsman, show a landowner a great hunt with your dogs, or offer to pay for hunting privileges.

Another tip: Go to your library and get the addresses of state, regional, and local chambers of commerce, then contact them for hunting leads. If possible, arrive a day or two early, head for the local courthouse or county Cooperative Extension service office (nearly every county in the country has one), and get a copy of the county plat book. Armed with this valuable information of who owns the land, find phone numbers and addresses in local telephone directories, then make a visit. Don't call first! It is far more difficult for a landowner

Asking landowners in person for hunting permission will improve your chances of gaining access to private property.

Homework starts at home. Planning a hunting trip for gamebirds is a fun part of the overall hunting experience.

to refuse access to a nonresident standing on his front porch than it is to say "No" over the phone.

Use the Internet. Type "pheasant" or "quail" and turn the search engines loose. All state departments of fish and game have Websites you can access. Simply type *http://www.dnr.state.mo.us/* for Missouri or *http://www.agfc.state.ar.us/* for Arkansas. You must know the proper name of the agency: "DNR," for example, stands for Department of Natural Resources. "AGFC" refers to Arkansas Game & Fish Commission. A handy guide is *Cabela's Wildlife Conservation Calendar* (800–237–4444), which comes out each year and lists the state agency Websites along with addresses and phone numbers. Included are particulars for Canadian provincial departments of fish and game, as well as outfitters and guides associations.

Many readers ask me about places I go to that I don't write about. They assume I have private stock somewhere or have privileged contacts that are off-limits to them. The truth is, I write about places anyone can visit. If I choose not to write about certain hunts, it is because the local resource can't take additional pressure or because access is prohibitive or because a guided hunt (which may have been complementary) was a bust. A question I get asked of-

After sizing up the available habitat and manpower, these grouse hunters are deciding who will hunt where.

To avoid surprises like this one, plan your hunting trip before you go.

ten is this one: "Tom, if you had a day left in your life to hunt pheasants (or quail or grouse), where would you go and why?" For the answers, read the "Ultimate Hunt" at the end of each section below.

PHEASANTS

They're making a comeback in states such as Minnesota, Wisconsin, and Michigan, thanks mostly to millions of acres of Conservation Reserve Program (CRP) land and some relatively mild winters in recent years. So look around in your own backyard to see if you have pheasants and your state has a hunting season (about 40 states do). But the big pheasant states—in respective order by hunter harvest—are usually South Dakota, Iowa, Kansas, and Nebraska.

In Iowa, concentrate in the central and northwest regions of the state—anywhere from 100 miles east of Des Moines—both north and south of I-80, down through Chariton to the south and up past Ames and Boone to the north.

South Dakota is the place to go for big numbers of birds, but getting access to private land is more difficult than ever unless you pay fees. It's worth paying, though, because many landowners realize their pheasants are an economic crop, and so they often arrange their farming and ranching practices around improving bird numbers. My advice is to hire an outfitter or go late in the season and knock on doors far from the popular Platte-to-Chamberlain region. There are public hunting areas in South Dakota, but they are hit hard, especially early in the season. Hunt them in the late season, when birds have filtered back from the crop lands.

I have enjoyed excellent pheasant hunting in North Dakota south of Bismarck and in the Flasher region, but the ranches are spread out and it's tough to find people at home. Northeast Nebraska usually has good numbers of birds, and they are found throughout Kansas except for the southeastern sector.

Ultimate Hunt: I'd choose eastern Montana, because if pheasants are under-gunned anywhere in America, it is probably here. Years ago, on a plains grouse hunt near Lewistown in September, I ran into more ringnecks than I could count in coulees and shelterbelts on private ranchland. A few years ago the best ringneck hunt of my life occurred on an Indian reservation in eastern Montana, which a pal and I were able to get on because my friend had a friend who knew someone. When we closed the car door, several roosters 100 yards away ducked their painted heads and skulked into the tall grass of a coulee. They didn't run away and they didn't fly, which told me they were not typical, prairie-bred, goosey

This brace of two-year-old ring-necked pheasants came from an Indian reservation in Montana.

ringnecks. My buddy and I shot six birds, and four of them sported spurs like small crabapple thorns—the mark of two-year-old, or older, birds.

QUAIL

Bobwhites are hunted in 30-some states, but in fringe places such as northern Indiana and southern Michigan they get slammed pretty hard by nasty winter weather. The top two states are typically Kansas and Oklahoma, which take turns leading the nation in annual harvest. I've had my best luck in southeastern Kansas and the Oklahoma panhandle. South and east Texas are also great in years with abundant rainfall. The same is true in Mexico, where friends of mine recently experienced an unbelievable day of 57 covey rises.

Ultimate Hunt: Western quail species, especially Gambel and scaled quail, have been providing great sport in recent years for hunters in Arizona and New Mexico. Both states have large tracts of Bureau of Land Management (BLM) properties, which are open to public hunting. Southeast Arizona and the Phoenix-to-Tucson region is good. In New Mexico focus on the southwest region west of I-25 and below Silver City. How well I remember a hunt a few years ago in January on BLM land in this general region. Four of us each bagged 15-bird limits.

Southwestern New Mexico was the setting for a mixed bag of Gambel (top) and scaled quail.

RUFFED GROUSE

Ruffed grouse hunting in Minnesota, Wisconsin, and Michigan has been very good in recent years, thanks to high populations in the cycles that span 10- to 20-year periods. These states annually lead the nation in harvests, which range, respectfully, from one-half million to a million birds each. Researchers believe the cycles are complex and not well understood. Reasons may include high numbers of predators, cold and wet springs that pinch off food production and kill chicks in the shell, and a parasite that plagues the species. However, even in poor production years it is possible to find pockets of grouse.

Vermont, New Hampshire, and Maine are other good states among the nearly 40 states where grouse are hunted. Upper New York State and western Massachusetts are also noteworthy most years. Pressure is highest in New England and certain areas of the upper Midwest. It is lowest in the West and Canada.

Ultimate Hunt: I never measure grouse success by the number of birds in the bag. To me a great day in the grouse woods is a dozen flushes, although in high-cycle years the figure could be 40 or more. My best day in the woods was 45 grouse and 15 woodcock flushed for only three hours of hunting. Friends of mine report days of 50 to 75 grouse flushes, although I have never experienced that many.

WOODCOCK

For the most part, woodcock breed east of the Mississippi River and north of the Mason/Dixon line. The best hunting is in New England and the upper Midwest in early to midfall. Once the birds begin migrating in October and November, hunting improves in Tennessee, Arkansas, and other southern states. It peaks in Louisiana, where most of the birds end up, in winter.

I keep accurate flush records on woodcock in Michigan, which is in the Central or Midwest Flyway where numbers have steadily declined since the late 1960s, when researchers began annual surveys. The breeding population has fallen about 40 percent in the past 30 years; consequently, the U.S. Fish & Wildlife Service (USF&WS) has reduced the daily bag limit to three birds here (the agency set a three-bird daily limit in the Eastern Flyway several years earlier). Hunting, incidentally, is compensatory and not additive to natural mortality, which is keyed largely to habitat loss.

Give a woodcock decent habitat and he'll increase the local population. Although only four eggs make a normal clutch, no bird recruits better than the woodcock. In spite of the general decline, pockets of good woodcock hunting remain, especially in Michigan, Minnesota, and Wisconsin.

Public land in these three states, which produce more woodcock than any other region in the country, is fairly abundant. Look for recently cut hardwood forests, especially aspen mixed with other young hardwoods and some pine. As

Some upland hunters claim ruffed grouse and woodcock are the number one and number two gamebirds. Or should that be the other way around?

these uplands freeze, woodcock move to lowland habitat, mostly alder runs and creek bottoms, which freeze last.

Ultimate Hunt: Although I believe that woodcock run more than many hunters realize, they still tend to hold better for dogs than most other upland birds. Those worn out from a long night of flying are especially reluctant to take wing again. If you ever chance upon a drop of flight birds that have traveled a long distance, you will know the hunting gods have smiled on you. It happened to me in northern Michigan several years ago. Flight birds having just crossed northern Lake Huron from Canada were resting in the first available Michigan habitat. My young setter made 35 productive points in an afternoon. I can still see her on point.

PLAINS GROUSE

Nothing beats a September hunt for plains grouse. Over the years I've had memorable experiences from September through December in North Dakota, South Dakota, Montana, and Nebraska for sharptails and in South Dakota, Nebraska, and Kansas for prairie chickens. Although at times you can post grainfields and pass-shoot incoming birds, I get a bigger tingle from walking the big, open prairies with my dog.

The best opportunities for South Dakota sharptails occur both up and down the west side of the Missouri River, which meanders through Pierre and evenly splits the state from north to south. The better chicken hunting is found from Pierre south to the Nebraska border.

Of the three national grasslands in South Dakota, only Fort Pierre, located in the state's central region, offers both types of plains grouse. The other federal properties—Grand River National Grassland near Lemon in the northwest region and Buffalo Gap National Grassland in the southwest—have sharptails only. Better opportunities for Kansas prairie chickens, though, occur in the Flint Hills region, but most of the land is private.

For Montana sharptails, try the bench and coulee country north and east of Great Falls. Ranchers in the area are pretty good about letting bird hunters on their land for reasonable daily lease fees. In North Dakota, hit the Missouri River breaks country between Bismarck and Garrison. There are good numbers of sharptails along the Little Missouri drainage, too, and I have hunted them successfully in the Badlands region around Beach and Medora.

I have hunted sage grouse in three of the nine western states where they are legal targets. For best opportunities, try BLM land in Wyoming's Shirley Basin north of Medicine Bow and in eastern Montana around Grass Range.

This South Dakota hunter proudly carries a sharp-tailed grouse and prairie chicken he shot on the public grassland near Pierre.

Ultimate Hunt: One September friends and I rented an old, wheezing Suburban at the Pierre, South Dakota airport and hunted both chickens and sharptails on the Fort Pierre National Grassland. There was a fine crop of birds, thanks to a near-double amount of rainfall that year. Our generous daily bags were evenly mixed with both species. One afternoon nine of us finished limits by taking birds from a rolling covey: As we shot our way up a hillside, birds kept flushing out all the way to the top and halfway down the other side. I think it used to be like that in the good old days of the late 19th century.

FOREST GROUSE

Besides ruffed grouse, hunters can target the blue and spruce species. Blue grouse are high mountain birds that can be hunted in Washington, Oregon, California, Nevada, Colorado, Idaho, Montana, Wyoming, Utah, and—to a lesser extent—New Mexico and Arizona. I have shot blues in Wyoming's

Shirley Basin, Nevada's Ruby Mountains, the New York range in Colorado, and the Little Belt Mountains of Montana.

Spruce grouse live in conifer forests at nearly any elevation across the continent. Once abundant in New England and the Great Lakes states, they are rarely seen in these areas because loggers removed their habitat a century or more ago. Seasons are closed in Michigan, Wisconsin, Maine, New York, Vermont, and New Hampshire. Except for Nova Scotia, they may be hunted throughout Canada and in Minnesota, Alaska, Idaho, Montana, and Washington.

To fully appreciate blue grouse and spruce grouse, you must hunt them with dogs. Otherwise, they seem unwary and offer little challenge.

Ultimate Hunt: In the Helena National Forest near Townsend, Montana one October afternoon, two friends and I flushed about 20 blue grouse over my Brittany. Although I am fairly sure these birds had never been hunted, they offered great sport, thanks to the dog. If my memory is right, I think we shot seven birds.

PARTRIDGE

If you've never hunted wild chukars, my advice is to work up to the sport or be in top physical condition before you go. Combing the 1,500-foot-high hills along Oregon's Deschutes River is physically demanding but not as tough as running around on the rimrock of Nevada's East Humboldt and Ruby mountains. Good chukar hunting is also available in Idaho, Utah, and Washington and in northeast and east-central California.

Hungarian partridge are found near ranches and farms in many western states. In Montana and the Dakotas, we have hunted them in the same haunts as sharptails, but you never really know where Huns will be. One time in Nevada, we ran into a covey in a mountain valley miles from the nearest human settlement. Some Midwest states have huntable populations of Huns, too, most notably northern Illinois and Iowa north of I-80.

Nevada's Ruby Mountains are the only place in North America to hunt the five-pound snowcock partridge, which is native to Afghanistan, Tibet, and Pakistan, and lives about as high above the earth as mountains grow. On a hunt with guide Bill Gibson of Elko, Nevada a few years ago, seven of us climbed to 10,000 feet and higher. Over five days we killed only two birds. Snowcocks are a real trophy, and you will never have a tougher bird hunt.

Ultimate Hunt: The best day I ever spent afield for chukars was with Gibson. We were hunting BLM land near Elko, and I was determined to stay up with him and his big-running Cheasapeake Bay retriever, Agate. The determination paid off with a six-bird limit. The only easy way to hunt chukars is on a gamebird farm, and that is no comparison with running and gunning for wild birds.

PTARMIGAN

There are three kinds of ptarmigan in North America—the willow, rock, and white-tailed species. The best places to hunt willow ptarmigan are in Quebec's Far North, northern British Columbia, the Northwest and Yukon territories,

Hungarian partridge offer spectacular hunting in several western states.

and Alaska. The rock ptarmigan's habitat often overlaps that of the willow, but it generally lives farther north and doesn't concentrate along rivers to the extent that the willow does.

The white-tailed ptarmigan is smaller than the bigger rock and willow species, which are about the size of small ruffed grouse. The white-tailed, an alpine bird that lives in the Rockies and other mountain ranges, is similar in size to a pigeon. The only white-tailed ptarmigan I ever shot was a Colorado bird I killed at just under 13,000 feet several years ago during a cross-country odyssey to take a North American grouse grand slam. California and Utah have limited hunting seasons. In Alaska you can hunt all three species.

Ultimate Hunt: I have yet to collect a rock ptarmigan, but I have enjoyed tremendous hunting several times for the willow species in northern Quebec near Kuujjuac, about 1,000 miles north of Montreal. On my first trip there in early September a few years ago, I hoped to find lots of birds for a young setter I had brought. Running out of shells (as did my two hunting partners), I turned to full-time training—staunching my dog, steadying

Tom Huggler and his setter, Sherlock, after a tiring but rewarding day hunting willow ptarmigan in Quebec's Far North.

him to wing, working on range with a long check cord. It was the best of all worlds.

DOVES

Thirty-nine states have mourning dove hunting seasons. Researchers estimate the fall continental population at 400 to 470 million birds, and hunters harvest about 10 percent of the total. Sixty-five percent or more of these migratory gamesters don't live long enough to return to the place where they were hatched, and so hunting has miniscule effect on the breeding population. The USF&WS regulates hunting seasons, which typically begin September 1.

Mourning doves are ubiquitous most years as long as food, water, and roosting cover are available. Their cousins, the white-winged dove and the band-tailed pigeon, are hunted in a handful of western states.

Ultimate Hunt: It is illegal to hunt doves in my native Michigan, and so I must travel to Indiana or Ohio to hunt them. I can think of no better way to spend

The climax to a well-planned hunt is being able to take a "success" photo, then enjoy the trip for years to come.

a September afternoon than to post a wheat stubble field just across the Michigan state line in Indiana and try to build a 15-bird limit at my feet before sundown. The sport affords great retriever training for my shorthair and a fine tune-up for my shooting eye during this first of all upland bird hunting seasons.

Planning any bird hunt is half the fun. Executing the plan is the other half. If you do it right and keep a notebook and take lots of photos, you can enjoy the experience over and over. Other chapters in this book offer more details on where to go and how to be successful.

CHAPTER
2

Choosing Guns, Chokes, and Loads

The 12-gauge shotgun is the most popular firearm in America for hunting upland gamebirds. Next is the 20-gauge, followed by the 16 and 28. Grouse and woodcock hunters seem to be fairly evenly split between 12s and 20s. Quail hunters favor the 20-gauge, pheasant hunters the 12. I see more double guns—both side-by-side and over-and-under models—in grouse woods than I do in pheasant sloughs, where autoloaders and pump guns tend to rule. Quail and dove gunners shoot them all, with perhaps autoloaders and pumps having a slight edge, especially among western quail hunters.

I have no statistics to support these observations. I can no more convince you which gauge and type of shotgun to buy than I can advise a Chevy truck over a Ford. I do, however, know what I like to hunt with and will share those opinions. Beyond that I suggest you shoot as many guns as time, money, and opportunity allow. The best decisions grow from informed opinion and experience.

I grew up shooting a 20-gauge Mossberg bolt action (the one with red and green safety tang) in modified choke. Later, as a high-school senior, I graduated to a 12-gauge Remington 870 pump with 30-inch, full-choke barrel. Thirty-five years later I still have that gun and enjoy shooting it and other pump models as well as autoloaders for waterfowl and the occasional dove hunt, but I have no use for them in the uplands. Two reasons: (1) most are too heavy to lug all day, (2) I don't want a third shot when I've already missed twice or have one, and sometimes two, downed birds to mark.

In upland habitats I prefer the double gun, but I'm no snob about it. After trying Red Labels and Browning Citoris and a Weatherby Orion, I now shoot pheasants and sage grouse and late-season prairie grouse with a 12-gauge Winchester Model 23, but I'm open to new experiences. I also shoot a Winchester Model 101 in 28 gauge and a Spanish side-by-side in 28 gauge. The 28, built on a true 28 frame, is ideal for the smaller birds from ruffed grouse down in size to partridge, quail, woodcock, and doves. They are good guns for doves and preserve birds and are a sensible choice for women and beginning shooters.

My interest in the 28 grew out of curiosity. On a Kansas pheasant hunt about 20 years ago, a friend noticed I was missing birds with my 870 pump, which contained a steel plug in the magazine to take up some of the recoil when I shot three-inch magnum shells at waterfowl.

Two ruffed grouse hunters discuss the merits of autoloader shotguns. This is a 20-gauge Franchi.

"Your gun is too heavy," he said (it weighed more than nine pounds). "Here, try my 20-gauge Citori."

I couldn't believe the difference in weight and the subsequent improvement in my shooting. Thus began my evolution toward lighter, smaller guns. I also changed tactics: hunting closer to my dog, anticipating the flush, passing up shots beyond 30 yards, trying to head-shoot the bigger birds like pheasants. I'll never be a great shot, but I have gotten better over the years for this and other reasons, which I'll explain.

THE ORIGIN OF CHOKES AND BORES

The introduction from France to England of pinfire breechloaders in the 1830s and the 1861 patenting of the centerfire primer by C. H. Daw completed the evolution from muzzleloading charges to percussion cartridges. During this period, bores (American shooters prefer the word "gauge") and chokes came under development and scrutiny. They evolved from the English proof houses, which date from more than 300 years ago, as a way of sizing barrels.

The bores get their names from the number of lead balls required to make one pound. For example, 12 lead balls that are each .729 inch in diameter equal

Hunting close to your dog and being ready for the flush will improve your score on pheasants and other upland gamebirds.

one pound, and that is why a 12-gauge gun has a bore diameter of .729 inches. A 28-gauge gun has a bore diameter of .550 inches, again, because 28 lead balls of that size are needed to equal one pound. The bore diameters for 16- and 20-gauge are .662 and .615 respectively. The .410, on the other hand, is measured in thousands, as are the rifle bores. Except in the hands of the most skilled shooter, the .410 has no place in the uplands—it simply is not enough gun.

The early English gunmakers made breechloading shotguns with various bore sizes. Besides the popular 12-, 16-, and 20-gauge barrels, 24, 28, 32, and other bores showed up. Greener, Powell, Macnaughton, Tranter, and Ford were among those who built 28-bore guns in the 1880s, and Ford in particular is credited with reintroducing the gauge after a period of absence. The earliest reference I could find to it was 1834 in the July issue of *Sportsman Magazine*. Then, as now, the 28-gauge was a misfit of sorts, and few shooters and hunters paid it any attention. Those that did, though, remarked as to its effectiveness. A *Rod & Gun* reader, writing under the pen name Priscus, in praising the 28-bore to good shots, had this to say: "Their lightness recommends them; and, although they seem toy-like, they afford as good sport, and fill the bag as well as larger and more cumbersome weapons."

Another proponent of the little gauge wrote to say that his friends stopped making fun of it and admitted its genuiness when they saw the gun perform: "I don't pretend to be a dead shot, although a fair shot, and I can say that I find I make quite as good work with the 28 as I used to with my 12s, and can kill my birds as clean and as far with the little gun as I can with a 12."

And why not? Guns in 12-, 16-, 20-, and 28-gauges are designed to throw the same size patterns at the same distances. Regardless of gauge, a full-choke gun is capable of placing 70 percent of its shot charge in a 30-inch circle at 40 yards. If the barrel is modified choke, 60 percent of the shot should fill the circle at 40 yards. Improved cylinder chokes will be 45 to 50

This traditional quail hunter prefers to shoot hundred-year-old hammer guns.

percent effective at that distance. Pattern densities will be thinner, however, with the smaller gauges, and that is why it takes a good shot to kill with them at long distances.

Further, given the smaller powder charge, there is usually less penetration—a second good argument for passing up those long pokes. The tighter the bore, the longer the shot column in the shotshell itself (1.210 inches for a 28-gauge as compared to .690 for a 12-gauge gun). As the shot pellets exit, barrel scrub or friction, then, is more pronounced in a smaller gauge gun. Higher gas pressures and more shot deformation, especially those pellets at the back end, result. In spite of these apparent deficiencies, though, the 28-gauge continues to perform well.

LOADS

Better shooters always think ahead to the day's hunting conditions and bring the right shotshells for the job. For example, when hunting woodcock in the early season, I carry No. 8 shot, which I find helps strain patterns in my skeet or improved cylinder barrels through heavy leaf cover. If grouse are mixed in, I'll stuff at least one tube of my double gun with No. 7½ shot. Later in the sea-

The over-and-under is popular among many kinds of upland bird hunters. This is a 20-gauge Citori.

son, when the screening cover and woodcock are gone and grouse are in full plumage, I'll switch to 7½ and 6 shot.

For quail, I like No. 8 or even No. 9 shot in a Winchester AA clay target load if gunning for preserve bobwhites and have also enjoyed success with Federal No. 8½ shot, especially for doves. For late-season plains grouse, which often flush wild, give me 6s because they have better downrange lethality than smaller, lighter pellets. Most 28-gauge rounds carry three-quarter ounce of lead, and Federal premium shotshells are copper-plated, which I like to use on adult birds in the late season. Winchester makes a one-ounce load in 28-gauge, which offers the knockdown power of a 20-gauge shell.

Limited to a single choice of shot size, I'll pick 7½ for all-round performance. Limited to a single choke, I'll select improved cylinder. For close-flushing pheasants, that combination is deadly in 12-gauge. Later in the season, I switch to 6s and even 5s and will reach for modifed/full choke tubes. I've experimented with hardened shot and find it helps penetrate gamebirds and kill them more cleanly. Some of the new no-lead alternatives, such as Bismuth and tungsten have a place in the uplands, although the shells are expensive.

Target loads are usually fine for smaller birds in the early season and field loads for most other times and conditions. As a general rule, you don't need magnum loads for upland birds. Exceptions are those five-pound sage grouse and snowcock partridge. You'll find that premium, brand-name shells are worth the extra money most of the time (sometimes cheaper, generic bargains work, too—it all depends on your gun).

No one hits every pheasant, quail, woodcock, or grouse they shoot at. On the other hand, no one likes to miss too often. Misses can lead to slumps. People could be watching. When game is scarce or hunting conditions are poor, you don't want to blow the scant opportunities the day offers. If you think about it, there is a reason for every shot missed on upland gamebirds.

Identifying the problem is the first step toward correcting it. Let's start with your gun.

THE IMPORTANCE OF GUN FIT

You wouldn't buy a suit off the clothing rack without trying it on first, and yet people purchase shotguns—some of them quite pricey—without a clue if the gun is the right fit for them. What to look for is a scientific and somewhat complicated process involving (1) length of pull (distance from trigger to center of heel plate, (2) cast (the amount of curve in the stock either toward the body—cast on—or away from it—cast off), (3) drop at heel and drop at comb (the bend of the stock downward from the barrel rib, and (4) other factors like balance and grip style. In the 19th century British gunmakers perfected an adjustable gunstock called the Try Gun to measure shooters to one-sixteenth inch of perfection. The theory and practice are similar to why a tailor determines precise body measurements before making a suit of clothing.

If you plan to spend more than $500 on a gun, you owe it to yourself to be Try Gun-fitted by a professional. This thinking is standard among Europeans; in America, it is just now coming into demand. Because Try Guns are expensive (as much as $10,000), only a few specialty gun shops have them (look for ads in such magazines as *The Double Gun Journal* and *Shooting Sportsman*).

I am now a strong proponent of gun fit. A few years ago, when I bought my Classic Doubles 101 (a Pigeon-grade Winchester) in 28-gauge, the first time I pulled the trigger I downed a sharp-tailed grouse at 57 yards. Later that day, in North Dakota, I went three for three on ring-necked pheasants—killing all three cocks with head shots as they were driven overhead from a shelter-belt. I love that little gun and continue to shoot well with it. Then, last fall I was Try Gun-fitted by Bryan Bilinski, who owns Fieldsport, Ltd. in Traverse

Proper gun fit is critical if you wish to become a competent wingshooter. Actor Jameson Parker tries his hand at sporting clays during the annual Quail Unlimited Celebrity Hunt.

City, Michigan. Armed with the certain knowledge of my exact measurements, I ordered a rather expensive 28-gauge side-by-side, a No. 2 from AyA in Spain.

The gun is an absolute delight, and my confidence has soared. On a whim, I asked Bilinski to measure my old 101. Would you believe it was within one-eighth to one-quarter inch of my precise measurements? In hindsight, I was lucky to have found such a good gun literally off the rack.

IMPACT TEST YOUR GUN

Most upland gunners are not not going to invest in a $150 Try Gun-fitting, let alone an expensive firearm, so what can they do? Answer: Impact test their guns. Set up a piece of cardboard at least 4 feet by 6 feet, paint a six-inch bull's-eye at eye level and measure 17 yards from the target to your stand. On a command of "Pull" or "Bird" from a partner, mount the gun quickly and smoothly as you would in the field. Do not aim (as with a rifle) but merely point at the bull's-eye and fire without hesitating. Do this at least a half-dozen times, changing the piece of cardboard as necessary. If most of your pattern is on or slightly above the bull's-eye, your gun is a reasonable fit. If your pattern

The author gets a shooting lesson from Bryan Bilinski, instructor at Fieldsport, Ltd.

is left or right, though, the stock needs to be cast on or cast off respectively. Shots far above or below the bull's-eye indicate problems with length of pull or drop at comb and heel.

You will probably be amazed (as I was) at what you learn. At the very least, the exercise may prompt you to learn more about gun fit and being tested for other problems, such as eye dominance, by a professional. There is a lot to learn here. In a two-hour videotape (*The Art of Shooting Flying*) Bilinski and I produced, we barely got into the subject.

IMPROVE MUSCLE MEMORY

One of the take-home lessons I learned in Bilinski's shooting school was that you can train at home to be a better wing shot. In any form of physical exercise, muscles retain memory through repetition. With your gun unloaded, stand before a mirror and practice mounting your gun through four simple steps:

1. *Stance* means pointing your left foot (if you're right-handed) at the break point of the target. Lean slightly forward to put the weight on this foot and prepare to pivot while swinging through.
2. *Ready Position* means holding the muzzle at a 45-degree angle (what most shooting instructors call "port arms"), finger on the trigger guard, and hitching the butt along the rib cage just under the armpit.

This hunter may appear to be in position, but the gun butt is too far from his rib cage.

This hunter is in a better position to hit the bird once it flushes.

3. *Mount* means bringing the gun to shoulder in one sparse movement, taking care to anchor your thumb under the cheekbone and not to move your head.
4. *Focus* on the target's leading edge means "painting through" the imaginary bird until you see daylight beyond its beak. And that's when you squeeze the trigger.

Later, in the comfort of your living room, practice mounting by following lines between wall and ceiling (horizontal shots) and wall and wall (vertical or rising shots). Doing this exercise 10 to 30 times daily, or until you tire, will help your muscles develop memory. In the field, you will then be on autopilot.

MATCHING LOADS TO CONDITIONS

Most guns pattern certain shells better than others. To find out, tack a piece of butcher paper to cardboard, draw a 30-inch diameter circle, back off 30 to 40 yards, and fire off a round. Count the number of pellets in the circle and divide by the number of pellets in the load (available from the manufacturer's catalog or Website) to get an efficiency rating. For example, 240 pellets in the circle from a total of 550 in the shell equals an efficiency rating of 44 percent.

Changing the paper after each round will help you determine which company's shells pattern best for shot size and drams of powder.

Remember, too, that choke dictates how patterns are made and, consequently, which shells work best in your gun. You may find one or two superior loads consistently pattern well throughout the choke regime. If so, replace chokes, not loads, for changing field conditions. If you own a favorite gun without choke tubes, consider having them added by a reputable company like Briley's.

POSITION YOURSELF

Unless you're hunting doves or posting a grainfield for prairie chickens or sharptails, you (or your partner or dog) have to flush your target in order to shoot at it. Because out of position usually means out of luck, you must learn to think ahead. Passive hunters carry home the shells they brought; aggressive hunters with a plan are the ones toting feathers at day's end. Which would you rather be?

Pheasants, grouse, quail, and even woodcock, run more today than ever before. Positioning yourself for the shot means identifying the likely places where a bird will flush and then being there when it takes to the air. Sample locations include pinch-points where cover peters out; the opposite side of a plum thicket, salt cedar, or willow thicket; and fingers of habitat that meander from the main cover and give a ringneck more running room. When hunting with a friend, one partner can cover the back door or escape route while the other flushes the bird.

CARRY YOUR GUN PROPERLY

No one can lug a six- to eight-pound gun all day at port arms—at least not without getting tennis elbow. But whether or not you carry the gun in a Butt Buddy holster or slung over your

Better shooters, such as actor Patrick Duffy, gain competence through practice and working on muscle memory.

Ready Position means carrying the gun at port arms and bringing your feet down on solid ground in anticipation of the flush.

shoulder, you should keep your trigger finger on the trigger guard and in line with the barrel. If you hunt with a dog, the time to move into the Ready Position, with your eyes over the gun muzzle, is when the dog is birdy. When we were filming a grouse hunting video a few years ago, my videographer learned to carry his camera on his shoulder, with thumb against the on/off switch. Because it takes 1.5 seconds for the camera to roll, he found that being ready was the only hope he had of capturing an exploding grouse on film.

I think about that often and then double-check my trigger finger and make sure my thumb is on the safety.

SIZE UP CONDITIONS

Gamebirds change patterns and habitats according to local hunting pressure, farming practices of grain harvesting and fall plowing, and changing weather conditions. As crops and screening cover go down, birds move into areas of greater security. Pheasants and quail, for example, invade cattail sloughs and marsh fringes. Woodcock often move to last-to-freeze lowlands, and grouse shift into conifers for protection. Where you found birds in September and October is not the place to look in November and December.

Learn to look at habitat for its current potential. Just as 90 percent of the fish live in only 10 percent of the lake, the same is true for upland gamebirds. I'll expand on this in the species chapters that follow.

WORK AS A TEAM

Having a good partner—two-legged or four-legged—to hunt with adds enormously to the joy of upland gunning. It can also help you to be successful, especially if you have developed teamwork. Using hand signals, for example, cuts down on needless noise. Seeing where your buddy is heading helps you to seal off the only escape route a pheasant has. I have learned to watch my setter's eyes when he is on point because invariably he will direct me to the frozen bird. Remember, too, that birds nearly always flush in the same direction a pointer or retriever is moving.

You need more than proper firepower to take birds. Understanding these other nuances, and looking for them in the field, will help you be a better bird shooter.

POSITIVE MENTAL ATTITUDE

The rest is up to you. In spite of doing all the right things, there will be days when the red gods conspire to send you home with deflated ego and flattened game bag. When that happens to me, I look at it this way: I had an enjoyable walk in the woods with good exercise and fine companionship. The birds I didn't get today will be there tomorrow.

CHAPTER
3

Selecting Clothing and Accessories

A few years ago I invited the outdoor writer of a major newspaper to go woodcock hunting with me in northern Michigan. He showed up totally overdressed, but no amount of advice from me could convince him to shed anything—not even his insulated vest or woolen ski cap. It was hot and dry that fall and I knew if we found any woodcock, they would be in heavy cover of alders and evergreens. We found plenty of birds, but my friend never got to shoot any because he was carrying half his clothing.

If you can size up conditions and dress just right for them, you will be comfortable. A comfortable bird hunter is a more effective predator.

THINK MINIMUM, NOT MAXIMUM

I think in terms of the minimum—what is the least amount of clothing I can wear and still be warm and dry? In early fall, that may be nothing more than lightweight hiking boots of Cordura and/or leather, a T-shirt, baseball cap, mesh vest, thin trousers with a bit of nylon facing, and lightweight shooting gloves. I go to rubber footwear, Jones cap, and rain suit when it is wet and a woolen ski cap, insulated boots, thin polypropylene underwear, and a shooting jacket when it is cold. In bitter cold weather, I'll slip on a facemask and heavier shooting gloves, especially on my left hand (I'm right-handed).

Last December I hunted grouse in sub-zero weather and wore medium-weight polypropylene underwear, woolen pants and shirt, insulated hunting coat, woolen ski cap, two pairs of woolen socks, and insulated Gore-Tex boots and gloves. A hood or trooper's cap with ear flaps might have made me

Because bird hunters create their own heat by walking so much, think minimum, not maximum, when it comes to clothing choices.

a bit warmer, but the handicap of not being able to hear birds flushing and losing peripheral vision was not worth the trade-off. As it was, I was plenty comfortable.

To my mind, the old saying of "you can always take it off" doesn't compute when you're hunting birds. Taking it off means I have to carry it.

LIGHTEN UP

That last thought segues into this one: The hunter who travels light can travel farther and will be less fatigued when birds go up. We bird hunters have an advantage over most deer and water-fowl gunners. Because we are ambula-

Cold weather prompted these pheasant hunters to don warm, bulky clothing.

It is not unusual for some bird hunters to walk 10 miles or more each day. The author takes a rest break during a hunt for sharp-tailed grouse.

tory, we help make our own warmth and comfort. Carrying only the essentials is a key part of comfort.

Figure it out: If you tote an extra pound of anything (heavy gun, too many shells, thermos of coffee, body fat, or clothing) and walk 10 miles (not unusual when plains grouse or Western quail are the quarry), you will needlessly move almost nine tons (1,760 steps per mile × 10 miles = 17,600 pounds).

Next time you lay out your hunting wear, put it on a bathroom scale, along with the other items you carry. You might be surprised. Fifteen pounds should be the maximum, unless you must lug water for yourself and the dogs (keep in mind, though, that one gallon equals six pounds) or the day is bitter cold and you need warmer clothing that may be bulky and heavy.

SYNTHETIC VERSUS NATURAL MATERIALS

A word about Gore-Tex: it is the best fabric we have for staying warm, dry, and windproof. It does need to be treated over time to maintain waterproofness of the outer shell, however, and I've found it a bit expensive.

Many old-time sportsmen stick with wool and for good reason. Wool has been around for thousands of years, and it has wonderful properties that cannot be matched by synthetics. Crush wool fibers thousands of times, and they still retain their natural shape. Soak them and they will absorb 30 percent of their own weight. Brush them against bark and branches, and they are surprisingly quiet. No wonder L.L. Bean and other companies continue to do a banner business in woolen outerwear.

Silk, cotton, and down are other natural materials that are ideal for undergarments and insulation (although cotton is not recommended as an undergarment in colder temperatures). There are dozens of synthetic fabrics available to today's bird hunters, and the manufacturers of underwear, outerwear, and footwear are finding new uses every day. Fleece garments, for example, help hunters stay quiet. Waterproof liners hung between inner and outer shells of jackets, parkas, coveralls, and pants keep them dry.

FROM HEAD TO TOE

The plethora of options doesn't mean everything available is well-suited to the bird hunter. Personally, I look for durable, lightweight clothing that is highly comfortable and will keep me dry and either warm or cool. In caps I prefer the low-fitting style without a button on the crown, to avoid having to pick them up when branches constantly knock them from my head. If caps don't offer a black or green under-visor to cut the sun's glare, I spray paint them accordingly. I like Jones caps the way they are—they make sense in wet weather because they drain water to the front and keep it off my neck.

In flannel shirts I prefer long sleeves with forearm protection if the garment doubles for outerwear. I look for tapered tails and a generous cut in the shoulders to avoid any binding when I swing through a target. I want pockets—on both sides of the breast if possible—and a penholder sleeve because I always tote a field notebook.

For belted trousers, I like loose but not baggy; otherwise, I have to wear suspenders, which all too often bind by day's end. I want rear pockets with button-down flaps, no leg cuffs please (they collect trash), but I usually need leg protection in two or three deniers of Cordura. When strolling a Southern plantation for bobwhite quail, I'll wear the lightweight pair; put me in chaparral for California quail and I'll need the heavier stuff.

Personally, I don't wear insulated trousers, because in cold weather I prefer to wear wool over polypropylene underwear, if necessary. Why? The stuff breathes, wicking away the perspiration that otherwise invades the trousers.

High-top leather boots allowed this bird hunter to hoof the miles between covey rises. A woolen sweater kept him warm; loose-fitting vest carried his essentials, but because it had no game bag, he had to improvise.

And wool breathes, too, plus it retains warmth when wet. Tightly woven wool can also turn back briars and even barbed wire. I learned to wear it during a sub-zero pheasant hunt in Kansas many years ago after blackberry tangles shredded my downhill ski bibs, which I had slipped on over long underwear.

I like a lightweight vest with nylon mesh that breathes for warm weather hunting and a full-fabric garment for colder days. Give me elasticized shotshell holders and Velcro cover flaps so I don't lose my cartridges. I want a roomy game pouch, one that expands cargo-style, is either detachable or zippers open fully for easy cleaning, and offers front and rear access. Ditto for coats, but also with Velcro cuff fasteners, a generous collar of corduroy or other soft material, and a waterproof yoke. I prefer raglan-style sleeves for maximum maneuverability. Some hunter orange in the yoke or sleeves is okay, but not on the entire garment.

FOOTWEAR

I read somewhere the typical person walks 65,000 miles in a lifetime. Because one-quarter of all the bones in the human body are located in the feet, shoes and boots that fit right are important. Footwear acts as a shock absorber and as a propulsion platform for moving forward, sideways, or backwards. Grouse hunters in particular know how important good footwear is. They spend hours walking up and down hills, over logs and windfalls, and through rugged, uneven terrain. But most upland hunters don't give footwear the critical consideration it deserves.

Tube socks and tennis shoes may be fine for posting a dove field in September. At other times, though, you'll be on the move, so begin by choosing boots that fit properly. If you can't go into the store and be properly measured by a skilled salesperson, trace your stockinged feet on a piece of paper and mail the outline with your order. A competent shoe salesman or factory representative will measure the longitudinal arch (distance from heel to ball of the foot) and the metatarsal arch (width from the knuckle of the little toe to the knuckle of the big toe) and send you footwear that fits.

What style is best depends on the type of bird hunting you do and when and where you go. I prefer leather footwear because the material breathes, and I can cinch the laces tightly for a snug, satisfying fit. I like an 8- to 10-inch-high boot with a Vibram sole that is moderately aggressive for a decent bite in most terrain. I want a rugged boot with double or triple stitching on the seams, extra sidewall support, and a toe guard to ensure long wear. Sometimes I'll even add Shoe Goo, a flexible hardening agent, to the toe for extra in-

The author prefers lightweight 10-inch-high leather boots that lace up on the lower half and use hook eyelets on the upper part.

surance in desert habitats where everything seems to cut and cling. Around the ankle/shin area, give me a soft collar, one that deflects trash, and add a finger loop on the upper back to aid in donning the boot.

Leather's drawbacks, by the way, are that it is not waterproof (silicone spray treatments notwithstanding) and that it can be heavy, depending on the construction.

For years I wore Bean's Maine Hunting Shoe and still have a pair the company rebuilt three or four times over the years. The lightweight combination of a leather upper and gummed-rubber bottom works especially well on wet ground that is level.

There is no perfect solution, I suppose. All-rubber boots retain moisture (the human foot contains thousands of sweat glands, which may secrete a cup or more of perspiration daily). They tend to be heavy and don't fit properly but can't be topped in wet weather. I keep a pair of 16-inch all-rubber Wellington-style boots in the back of my truck but can't wear them day after day. My feet grow sore; the heels of my socks wear away. A better choice is a

Gore-Tex boot. Again, Gore-Tex is a bit more expensive, and you'll still have to treat the leather like your other boots.

I want lightness in a boot—no more than two pounds each in a leather model—unless I am hunting rimrock talus for chukars or other high country habitats for white-tailed ptarmigan or mountain quail. Then, extra weight affords increased stability. One way to add weight is through an aggressive sole. Another is by wearing an insulated boot.

The answer to the question "What boot is best?" lies in personal choice. A fellow I know hunts mountain quail in Nevada while wearing Nike running shoes and does just fine. Another swears by his $400 rubber boots made in France. Yet another, who has a foot deformity, says his specially-made Russell boots are the only footwear that keeps him going. Each is correct, of course, and yet there are things, besides getting properly fitted, that all bird hunters can do to achieve the ultimate in comfort and efficiency.

Break in your boots. Another friend of mine also prefers leather footwear. After lacing up a new pair he stands in a pail of water, then walks until the boots begin to dry, claiming he gets a better fit. I've never tried this tactic, perhaps because I don't have the courage to soak a brand-new pair of $200 boots. I do know, however, that wearing new footwear in the field is a recipe for disaster. Gently break in the boots by wearing them around the house an hour or two each day for a week or so before the hunt. At the end of the first day of hunting European woodcock in the Republic of Ukraine a couple of years ago, I watched one of my companions swab blood from his new boots. His blistered feet troubled him every day of the six-day-long hunt.

Layer your socks. You should wear two pairs of socks. Most cotton tube socks worn next to the skin are comfortable at first, but they absorb moisture and then retain it—just like a terry cloth towel. Pretty soon they feel clammy and ball up underfoot. Unbleached cotton socks are a better choice but hard to find. Instead, begin with a thin polypropylene or silk stocking, which will wick away moisture and pass it to the outside. The outer sock should be wool or acrylic or a blend of the two. Hollow-core fibers also draw moisture and release it to the boot. Better socks have reinforcement in the balls and heels of the feet.

Change socks at midday. Give your feet a break at lunch time each day. Then change boots every day. You'll feel refreshed and hunt more comfortably.

Lace tightly. I like footwear with four or five eyelets in the bottom and quick-lace fasteners above. I pull the laces as tightly as possible to the instep, then tie a square knot to hold the tension. After flexing my foot forward a few times—to ensure blood circulation—I finish lacing and tie a double knot, which will discourage unraveling. Folding over your socks also helps.

ACCESSORIES

Several other clothing and accessory considerations can contribute to a smooth bird hunt. I keep a pair of chaps, for example, in the large plastic tub that goes with me in my pickup truck on every bird hunt. They'll turn back everything but the nastiest cacti spines, and they slide on quickly over blue jeans or other pants. Sometimes I wear them in early morning when fields are wet and I don't need rainwear but want to stay dry.

Change socks at midday and boots every day for maximum comfort if you plan to walk a lot.

Like boots, I have yet to find rain-wear that is perfect for hunting birds. Gore-Tex bibs, coats, and trousers have been improved lately by L.L. Bean, but I haven't had a chance to test them in the field. If they are as tough, waterproof, and breathable as they say, I am certainly in favor of it. I've gone through a few waxed cotton coats in my lifetime, but they are not warm (unless worn over a sweater) and must be treated periodically to remain waterproof. In time, the brambles get to them, too. Over the years, I've come to rely on rubber. Invest in the better stuff made for sailing and boating. Dress lightly, though, or sweat yourself into a lather.

A good pair of hip boots belong in the clothing arsenal of the bird hunter, especially the pheasant enthusiast who goes after late-season birds in cattail marshes where they go to escape predators and bad weather.

I used to shun gloves when bird hunting because most types are cumbersome at best. Then I discovered shooting gloves, a natural outgrowth of gloves developed for baseball players and golfers. I found I could eliminate the roadmap of hand scratches that gave mute but grim testimony I had been in the grouse tangles. Now that I've upgraded my gun cabinet to include a good (i.e. expensive) double gun or two, I don't like marring the barrels with fingerprints. So, I bought an ultra-thin pair of leather shooting gloves and

Chaps are an important item to consider in cactus country.

liked them so well I picked up a second pair containing a bit of Thinsulate for cold weather hunting. These days you'll rarely catch me barehanded in the woods.

You should invest in protective eyewear to help ensure against injury. Any grouse or woodcock hunter who claims to have never taken a poke in the eye from a twig or a slap across the face from a sprung sapling or berry cane either has a short memory or isn't hunting where birds are found. Put shatterproof eyewear in the same league as fluorescent orange clothing for insurance against a hunting accident. No gunner should go afield without it, and there are plenty of styles, colors, and models on today's market.

I never enter unfamiliar woods without checking my compass. As Global Positioning System (GPS) electronics come down in price and weight, they appear more attractive to me. Even if I buy one some day, though, I'll probably still carry my compass, which I wear on the lanyard that contains my bird flush counters, dog whistle, and spare key to the pickup. I don't care for the pin-on compass although many hunters I know rely on them. I've never found the pin-style to be as dead-on accurate as a sensitive pocket-style compass, and I'm always concerned that a branch will pop open the pin and strip the compass away. Pocket items tend to get lost, too, though, and that is why the compass goes around my head.

The best dog whistles I've found are those that contain a pea-sized ball—something other than a ball bearing, which seizes up in cold weather and turns your "come back" call into a reedy whimper. Because I often hunt with friends whose dog whistles sound a lot like mine, I keep a variety of other locators on hand. For years I have tallied grouse and woodcock flushes on separate bead-style counters, which you can buy with or without whistles from dog supply houses such as Dunn's or Scott's. I enjoy keeping score so much that I now mark rooster pheasant flushes and quail coveys.

Other accessories a bird hunter must consider taking afield include electronics such as beeper locators and shock collars for your dog. Excellent choices are available, and you can get both in a single unit, complete with controls the handler wears around his neck. If you plan to carry a hand-held transmitter, put it in a secure holster rather than drop it in the game bag where it can get lost or set off accidentally.

One of these days for Christmas or Father's Day, I'm going to ask for a specialty bird hunting knife, the kind that has a folding gut hook. This feature is especially useful if you draw your birds in the field. I seldom do (unless the day is hot) because I like to age my birds in the truck cooler or refrigerator at home. I do, however, carry a small pocket knife for this purpose and any exigency that comes along. Again, with an eye to weight, I carefully select other items to carry. This typically includes a handkerchief, roll of hard candy to keep my mouth wet, small pair of pliers/wirecutters for dog encounters with porcupines and predator snares, and a tube of Nutri-Cal for my dogs if I'm going to be out several hours and the weather is cold. This high-energy treat is a hedge against hypothermia. I didn't have any on me one cold day in Kansas a couple of years ago when a friend's setter went down. A butterscotch candy helped the dog back on his feet, but we had to quit the hunt and fetch my friend's four-wheel-drive truck to rescue the dog.

Other personal items to consider are a bottle of water for you and your dogs and a camera.

PACKING YOUR VEHICLE

Develop a checklist for gear you might need in the field. Each time you think of something, add it to the list, then consider everything before leaving home. Here are the items I typically pack for an upland bird hunt:

General items
Sleeping bag
Hypothermia blanket
Spare clothes, boots
Spare boot laces
Knife
Choke tubes and wrench
Clipboard, pencils

These South Dakota bird hunters enjoy a field lunch, with all the comforts of home.

Shooting glasses

Binoculars

Water, food

Maps

Flashlight

Toolbox

Gun cleaning kit

First-aid kit

Cooler for birds

Shells

Gear for Dogs

Dry towels

Chains

Extra leashes

Food, treats

Water pail with lid

Food and water bowls

Kennel cover

Beeper collar

Bells

Needle-nose pliers (for porcupine quills and cacti spines)

Dog whistles

Rubber footwear (yes, dog boots)

First-aid kit

CHAPTER
4

Hunting With and Without Dogs

O ne cold, windy afternoon in January some friends and I were lounging in a restaurant in Rock, Kansas, in the heart of the Flint Hills, picking at the crumbs of apple pie on our plates, drinking coffee, killing time. We were en route to post a grainfield where prairie chickens had been feeding in late afternoon. There was no hurry, so we stopped for lunch.

The idle talk turned to bird dogs.

Outside, in the Suburban, the dogs slept, and the bobwhite quail we had killed that bitter morning grew stiff with cold.

"You should have seen that point Rex made," one of my friends said. "Snapped to like he was hit in the face."

"He *was* hit in the face," another offered. "With the scent of 20 bobwhites coming down that wind tunnel, you'd snap to yourself. If you could smell 'em, that is."

When the subject is bird dogs, everyone has a story or an opinion or both. Someone told the tale of how a man cured gun shyness in a pointer by devising ear plugs for the dog. Another friend mentioned how you could repair a cut paw by applying a drop or two of Krazy

We all have our dog stories, or opinions, or both.

Glue to a small piece of newsprint and laying it over the torn pad. The glue acts as a temporary suture and wears off about the time the cut has healed.

A third recalled how one of the best grouse dogs he ever hunted over was a Labrador retriever from Minnesota. "You just can't beat a Lab," he added.

"Or a good springer spaniel, especially for pheasants," I said.

"Well, have you ever hunted behind a Chesapeake Bay retriever?" said the fellow who had told the glue story. "I have and they're Sherman tanks when it comes to busting tough cover."

WHAT MAKES A GOOD HUNTING DOG?

Leaning back in my chair, I wondered aloud what my companions, two of whom were professional dog trainers and guides, look for in a bird dog.

"A birdfinder," one of them said. "He has to know where to locate birds."

"And hold them, if he's a pointer or setter," the other said. "I mean, hold 'em while you go and have lunch. Come back an hour later and that dog better be rock-solid."

A third opinion: "A good pointer always honors another's points. He'll hunt aggressive but he won't be a me-firster. If he's a flushing breed, I want him lacing my boots, not out there gobbling ground in the next county."

We argued the merits of steadiness to wing and shot in pointing breeds and the alternative—letting the dog get a running start on the retrieve. Then we debated qualities all breeds should exhibit such as biddability, endurance, and good temperament. Everyone agreed that a good birder will be full of fire but no rebel—you won't need an Allen wrench to tighten the bolts in his head. The dog will possess the physical confirmation to hunt all day and come back for more, and he will have the heart to do the job for you. The perfect

The Chesapeake Bay retriever is more than a waterfowler's dog. One that is well-trained is a delight in the uplands.

partner will be a wonderful family pet with a pleasing, loving disposition and one that is good with kids.

So, what breed do you own? What kind of dog should you buy? I could no more tell you that than to suggest a blonde for a wife over a brunette. The answer lies in the kind of hunting you do and the type of personality you have and are looking for in a hunting partner. Besides the black and yellow Labradors, golden retrievers, shorthairs, Brittanys, and the many setters who have stolen a piece of my heart, I have hunted with Gordon setters, Irish setters, vizslas, various wire-haired breeds, Weimaraners, Munsterlanders, a Braque Francais (all pointing breeds), as well as Chesapeake Bay retrievers, springer spaniels, Boykin spaniels, and cocker spaniels (flushing breeds). Some were good; a few were great. Each was memorable in his or her own way, and I could write a book on the subject.

PICKING A PUPPY

If you've never owned a hunting dog, start with an easy-going golden or Labrador retriever. They naturally fetch, typically are mild-mannered around children, and often are easier to train than many individuals within the pointing breeds. Weeks 6 to 12 in a puppy's life are prime transition time for attachment to people. If the dog you are planning to buy has had sufficient human contact before it reaches 12 weeks, the animal should have no problem bonding to you.

You're paying for good breeding, so ask to see a pedigree. At the very least, it means the breeder cares enough to keep records. Ask the breeder for references and to see the parents in person. It's even better if you can hunt behind one or both. Then, make your own evaluation: Would you like to own the parents of the puppy you are considering?

How solicitous is the breeder toward his animals? Is he feeding premium, brand-name food or bargain-basement junk that comes in oily bags? Look around. Is the bedding clean and is water always available? Do you get the feeling raising pups is a chore to him or a fun job? How sure is the breeder of his product—sure enough to produce shot and worming records, a health certificate and registration papers for the American Field Publishing Company's *Field Dog Stud Book?*

If you're paying $500 or more, insist on certificates of guarantee for the parents from the Orthopedic Foundation for Animals and the Canine Eye Registration Foundation and a six-month guarantee against hip dysplasia

The human bonding period is 6 to 12 weeks of age for a puppy. These Labrador retriever pups have a whole new world of bird hunting to discover.

and hereditary defects (the guarantee is a full refund or free pick from the next litter).

Picking a puppy is never easy if you listen purely to your heart and go for looks. I once sold a setter puppy to an artist friend who went strictly for beauty. "Cleo" had two black eye patches and was one of the lovliest pups I had ever seen. Because she had an aggressive disposition, I advised my friend—a first-time dog owner and the father of young children—to pick another pup. He insisted on buying Cleo, then returned her a week later because his kids were afraid of her. Who could blame them? The pup had bitten them.

PUP, STARTED DOG, OR FINISHED PARTNER?

Anyone who ever wanted to own a hunting dog has asked the question, "Should I buy a pup or started dog?" Sometimes we wonder if a finished dog is the best answer. Consider time of year. Although I'll take a puppy hunting at any age it shows interest, the most I can hope for is an introduction to the gun, bonding with me, and maybe a mouthful of feathers. Every dog has its

Dogs that are bred to hunt live for the experience. This yellow Labrador retriever enjoyed hunting for bobwhite quail.

own "readiness" time clock. If you want to be sure of a hunting partner this fall, buy a started dog—a 6- to 18-month-old that knows basic commands and has proven its interest in game. Instinct does not take the place of training, and a started dog should show definite signs of both. Expect to pay two to three times the price of a pup.

A finished gun dog can easily cost twice again the price of a started dog, or four times that of a pup. A finished dog is at least two years old and preferably three or four. The dog's age and talent dictate price. Beyond age five your investment loses some of its attraction because a bird dog's prime years mostly fall between three and eight years.

I go with a pup whenever possible. You learn the dog's personality as the animal grows. It becomes part of the family, and—just like kids—having a pup around has a strange way of turning back the clock on your own age.

INVEST IN A TRAINER

A good dog is the best investment a hunter can make. The only way to get the maximum dividend from that investment, however, is to see the animal is fully and properly trained. You owe that much to the dog; it is your part of the bargain. Begin by teaching basic obedience commands: Whoa, Stay, Come, Heel, Kennel, Down, Fetch, Give. You should be able to do this yourself. Buy a good book on training (there are several; ask a trainer to recommend one), or enroll in a community education class. If you're new to the game, do both.

I've never paid a professional trainer to teach my dogs these simple commands. Doing it yourself helps establish you as Alpha (leader of the pack) and creates a bond of trust and consistency with your dog.

After you've done that, take the dog to a competent trainer for an evaluation of the dog's ability and willingness to hunt birds. The trainer will have the experience and the tools—including gamebirds—to take the dog to the next level, assuming the breeding is there for him to work with. Most dogs will transfer the ownership bond from you to a qualified trainer and back again, although some breeds (most notably Chesapeake Bay retrievers and some wire-haired pointers) and certain individuals of any breed may require more time.

I rely on professional trainers to introduce my young dogs—typically between the ages of eight months and two years—to birds and to teach them how to handle them properly. The rest is up to me come hunting season. A two-week tuneup at the trainer's the following summer is the clincher for checking problems with ranging, staunchness,

Begin by teaching the basic commands, such as whoa, heel, and come.

Investing in a professional trainer is the best way to realize the full potential of your hunting partner. This English setter is learning how to retrieve.

Finding birds in this ocean of grass would be a tall order without this experienced English setter.

Successful hunter with a pair of bobwhite quail. Would he have found more birds by relying on a good dog? Yes!

steadiness to wing and shot, and retrieving. It is also a hedge against the boldness many dogs exhibit in their second or third year.

The $500 or so I spend on training is money well invested. A dog that lives 10 years will likely cost $5,000 when you add up vet bills, food, training paraphernalia, boarding fees, dog boxes, kennel, and more. That $500 training bill amounts to only about 10 percent of the total outlay and is the best assurance for realizing the dog's full potential.

HUNTING WITHOUT A DOG

Dogs add so much to the joy of bird hunting that I can't imagine heading into the woods, mountains, or fields without one, regardless of who owns the animal. I've never had a period in my life where there were no dogs to hunt with, but I acknowledge that many people hunt birds without them. My late friend, Carl Parker, shot more than 600 ruffed grouse over a 30-year hunting career in New York and never owned a dog because he traveled a lot and lived in apartments. Lawrence Smith and Carl Tucker, friends of mine from Elkhart, Kansas, have hunted lesser prairie chickens and bobwhite and scaled quail together for some 60 years. Neither has ever owned a four-footed partner.

These gentlemen were a joy afield because they appreciated my dogs and didn't interfere by trying to manage

How many pheasants will this dogless hunter walk past? We'll never know.

them. When afield with other dogless hunters, though, I have witnessed shabby behavior toward owners and their charges.

Most hunts, certainly those involving a drive, need a huntmaster, but some people seem unwilling to take directions. Others are ignorant, especially if they don't know much about dogs. We all know what happens when one man makes a derogatory comment about another man's wife or girlfriend. Even if the obligatory fistfight does not ensue, a friendship will be strained and perhaps damaged forever. Would you believe the same result can occur over impromptu comments made about someone's hunting dog?

Assume, for example, that you are having dinner at a friend's house and the meat loaf is a bit tough. You would hardly tell your friend's wife that her specialty would gag a zoo monkey. By what logic, then, would you comment that so and so's wide-ranging pointer could outrace any greyhound on earth or his retriever has suet for brains? Much better to say, "Rocket's a young dog, isn't he? I've been told some pointers (or retrievers) can be hard to handle."

Then, if you must roll your eyes, first turn your back.

Courtesy and common sense should always prevail when going afield with another's dogs. Here is a 10-point plan of etiquette to consider:

1. *Refrain from Giving Commands.* The dog is likely trained to follow one set of rules from one person, and even if you think you understand orders like "Come," "Heel," "Hunt Dead," and "Fetch," don't succumb to the temptation. Especially in a hunting situation (as opposed to relaxing after the hunt), the dog will most likely ignore you, and then what do you do? Some owners talk constantly to their dogs, others say little or nothing, and a few rely entirely on whistle commands. Anything you say, therefore, confuses the dog. If the owner wants you to give commands, he'll tell you.

2. *Resist the Temptation to Lecture or Criticize.* Let me be blunt: Keep your opinion to yourself. You are not paying the bills nor do you have the responsibility for the dog. If you know a great deal about training dogs, or the behaviorial characteristics of this breed, or the sex and age idiosyncrasies of this particular bloodline, then maybe your observations are valid and worthy of comment. Even so, let the owner ask before offering. No one knows the dog like his owner and even though the owner might be short-sighted, it's still his privilege to ask for an opinion if he wants it.

3. *Respect the Owner's Investment.* Like his gun, his car, and his hundred-year-old Parker, the owner's dog is an investment to be realized. Most hunting dogs contribute something valuable, unless the animal is completely untrained. Knowing how expensive a hunting dog can be might help you to appreciate what the dog does right. Keep in mind, too, that every dog has a bad day afield, and that day will probably begin within an hour of the owner bragging about his wonderful four-footed partner.

4. *Factor the Emotional Attachment.* Every parent thinks his kid should be a starter on the soccer team. That's why what you—the hunting guest—see as spoiled behavior is considered "personality" by the owner. What you are sure is lack of discipline is "immaturity." Although I'd rather you didn't evaluate my dogs' weaknesses, I know I'm too close to do it fairly myself. That's why I insist on a no-holds-barred report card from my trainer. He is the professional.

5. *If You Must Correct, Ask First.* Because a dog is poorly trained or undisciplined does not mean that you must put up with muddy paws, hair in your coffee mug, or Alpo breath in your face. Dogs should not jump uninvited into cars with open doors. They should never be underfoot when it comes time for cleaning birds, and—horror of horrors—they should not be allowed to get into the lunch or even to beg for it. When these things happen, tell the owner. Ask him to manage his dog, or—if all else

Southwestern quail hunters strongly rely on the Brittany.

fails—ask permission to do the correcting yourself. Other questions the dogless hunter might ask include:

Is it okay if I give your dog a snack? Is he steady to wing? To shot? Should I move in on his points or wait for you? Do you mind if I shoot rabbits over your bird dog? Should I take retrieved birds or let him bring them to you? Do we shoot only over points? Anything else I need to know?

6. *Respect a Dog's Space.* A friend once told me that a setter bitch I owned was dangerous. "I've never had a dog try to bite me when I reached in the kennel like that," he said. That dog had faults all right, but being mean-spirited or dangerous was not one of them. The man tried to coax the dog from her warm box in the back of my truck one cold winter morning. When she refused to budge, he reached in to collar her and she snapped at him. Because most dogs are territorial, they protect their kennel, yard, garage, or other space alloted to them. Once again, let the owner handle his dog.

7. *Never Ask to Borrow Another's Dog.* And if someone offers to let you take his dog hunting, be ready to assume full responsibility. A yellow Lab I once owned would hunt well for anyone, was a joy to handle, and never caused a problem. No professional had ever worked with her, and so the extra experience she gained by my loaning her to trusted friends was

Bobwhite hunters typically prefer pointing breeds, such as this English pointer.

Or this English setter.

The golden retriever is a fine companion for all-around upland hunting. This one has just retrieved a scaled quail.

good for her. On the other hand, a well-trained setter I let someone borrow one time came back with steadiness problems because the handler was either lax or didn't know what to do.

8. *Accept the Fact That Some Dogs are One-Man Dogs.* One time on a pheasant hunt with two hard-charging Chessies, the only way I could get a shot was to tramp right along with the owner. The dogs put up plenty of birds for him, and I, too, got to share in the success. Had I not figured out the program, I would have been birdless.

9. *Allow the Owner to Run the Hunt.* On the other hand, most

flushing or pointing breeds that are trained to do so will hunt for the line of hunters. Taking the center, the owner sets the pace and tells everyone how far out on the wings to travel. If you are one of the dogless hunters, avoid the temptation to move the hunt along or to cover ground that is out of bounds, so to speak. The farther a dog must run the line, the less secure are the "wires" between dog and owner.

10. *Never Punish Another's Dog.* Dogs do bizzare things when excited or in strange surroundings. A Brittany I once knew trashed the interior of a friend's truck when he and the dog's owner went into a restaurant for lunch. The owner (who should have known better) and not the dog was to blame, so why punish the dog? Besides, you might lose a finger in the process.

Although you can have fun hunting birds without dogs, having one or more along enhances the sport. You'll likely find more game, both live and dead. You'll be part of a bigger drama that now has a prologue (the find) and an epilogue (the retrieve), thanks to the dog. Maybe that's why years later I may well have forgotten some of the people I hunted with, but I almost always remember the dogs.

CHAPTER 5

The Ruffed Grouse

There is no middle ground when it comes to ruffed grouse hunters. They either take their "pats" or "partridges" incidentally when after pheasants or rabbits, or they seek them on their own merits with a peculiar kind of fever. These dedicated hunters often invest in fitted guns, well-trained dogs, premium shells, specialty clothing, even four-wheel-drive vehicles—all in the pursuit of what they claim is the king of the upland gamebirds. I am not one to argue, having grown from one extreme of hunter to the other.

I pouched my first "ruff" as a sort of accident while tracking rabbits around Sand Lake in Iosco County, Michigan, many years ago. Since that time the memories of whirring wings, the tang of gunpowder, the love for a bird so handsomely designed, have worked like a potion to make grouse hunting as close to an obsession as I dare allow.

It is amazing how storm windows can lie waiting in the cellar and how quickly fallen leaves accumulate on the lawn during grouse hunting season. And because woodcock are often found in similar habitats, we grouse hunters get a bonus bird. In fact, a growing number (myself included) target woodcock first and consider grouse to be the perk—that is, until the woodcock leave

Many upland hunters proclaim ruffed grouse the king of all gamebirds.

the north country. Then we rediscover grouse and fall in love all over again.

HUNT THE HABITAT FIRST

When I began hunting more than forty years ago, the woods all looked alike. Although it is true that grouse can be found nearly anywhere during the "fall shuffle" as juveniles move to claim new territories, I have learned that habitat niches attract and hold birds. I began to understand this phenomenon when I found good shooting in certain covers and then made mental notes of what those covers contained. Now, not only can I piece together prime covers from the mind images of thousands I have seen, but also, on occasion, I can smell good grouse woods.

For many grouse hunters, the season unofficially opens on October 1, about the time the maples and other hardwoods are turning color.

Grouse will live out their lives in 40-acre habitats if their life-cycle needs are met. A pair of hunters took these birds from prime cover.

If your nose leads you, for example, to fermented fruit and berries, you will often find grouse there or nearby. That little patch of hawthorns brings to mind a similar thicket years ago that was full of birds. A solitary aspen in a small swarm of pine was a favorite perch for another bird at another time.

It pays to know that grouse are highly sensitive to their home turf, and what passed as excellent cover last year may decline to mediocrity the next and may well be worthless in another year or two. A grouse will spend his entire life in some 40 acres of woods if those woods contain drumming logs (for males), heavy density of aspen saplings (for nesting hens), a canopy of security cover from hawks and owls, and food.

Grouse cover is usually thick. Young aspen (also called poplar, popple, or slashings) aged 10 to 20 years is a favorite because wintering grouse eat the large, nutritious male buds and the typically heavy stem density protects the birds from raptors. Grouse also use mixed habitats of hickory, oak, birch, and other hardwoods seamed with pine, spruce, and other conifers. Although found in wilderness, they are not necessarily a wilderness bird, having adapted well to fragmented habitats in public forests as well as Western drainages and Eastern rural and sometimes suburban woodlots.

Age diversity almost always makes for good grouse habitat. The only way to ensure it is to manage the forest by selective cutting practices. The removal of mature timber allows sunlight to reach the forest floor where ground cover and understories to conifers, aspens, and other hardwoods grow. The understories include gray, silky, and red osier dogwood; witch and beaked hazel; and caned fruit such as blackberry and raspberry. Other good foods are wild grapes, crabapples, hawthorns, highbush cranberry, autumn olive, acorns, beechnuts, wild cherries, and other forms of mast. Closer to the ground, grouse love clover, rose hips, wintergreen berries, and mushrooms. Old apple orchards gone to seed are good places to find birds. These are all foods I have found in the crops of grouse killed in the upper Great Lakes region.

Grouse habitats may be large or small. This New Hampshire covert is tiny by upper Midwest standards.

A New York study of grouse crops found 65 different plant families totaling more than 400 actual species, although the birds' preference was aspen buds and flowers, followed by clover leaves and hazelnut buds. Other studies proved that Virginia grouse of the Allegheny Mountains liked acorns, grapes, and greenbrier fruit and leaves. In Ohio, they preferred not only greenbrier and aspen but also the fruit of gray dogwood, as well as beech buds, wild grape, and sumac.

Birds of the Pacific Northwest have different preferences. In Idaho they liked sedge followed by blueberries. In Washington State they preferred buttercup, then black cottonwood, gooseberries, and blackberries. On Vancouver Island researchers found the birds stuffed with salal fruit.

Find the food and find the grouse. This bird was eating highbush cranberries, which carry fruit well into winter.

Opportunistic feeders, grouse usually turn to green matter, fruit and acorns, or other mast in September. In October and November, they rely more heavily on apples and other fruits. Then in winter they turn to ground cover foods such as wintergreen and rose hips. And they gorge themselves on the buds and catkins of aspen and other trees. Tough birds, they can digest poison ivy berries and leaves, toxic laurel mountain leaves, poisonous nightshade berries, even cockleburs and burdock.

A good tip is to pick up a shirt-pocket size paperback or two on tree, shrub, and wildflower identification. Also, check the crops of birds you kill. One morning a few years ago, for example, I found beechnuts in the bulging crop of my first kill of the day. I knew of a beechnut forest less than 200 yards away and, yes, it was full of birds. Another tip: Be versatile and learn to hunt in many places, eliminating the unproductive ones. A retired friend, for example, has about 75 key coverts that he hunts each year. He calls them his "friends." He substitutes those that have grown to maturity and no longer hold grouse for new spots, which he is constantly discovering.

Learn to hunt habitat first, then look for grouse. Some of your hunting can be done via the telephone or Internet by inquiring of state and federal foresters the location of logging operations.

In most New England states, habitats tend to be smaller than in Maine, New Brunswick, Nova Scotia, or any of the upper Midwest states where I have hunted. On a typical day in Michigan, for example, I may visit four coverts, but in Vermont or New Hampshire I'll hit at least twice that many. It might take only twenty minutes to drive to a certain apple orchard in Vermont and another ten minutes to find out if a grouse is home. Grouse hunters in western states typically hunt high country drainages with aspen or belts of aspen below the conifer timberline.

But to really understand grouse, you need to hunt them under all conditions. You will learn, for example, that birds sit tightly on wet, rainy days and become jittery and flush wildly on windy days. In time, you will learn to watch the trees as well as the ground, and if you are like the rest of us converts, will shamelessly rake a bird or two from limbs before insisting that all shots in the future be taken on the wing.

You will also watch your shooting scores improve from the tight foliage of September to the leaf drop of late October, then see them perhaps plummet again in December when birds seek the evergreen cloak of safety in swamp growth and pine plantations.

LEARN THE THREE SEASONS

Grouse seasons in many states begin in September and run well into winter. Within these long seasons are actually three separate mini-seasons. Each has its good and bad points. For example, in September, grouse can be anywhere because food supplies are more abundant than at any other time of year. Further, the heavy ground cover of green bracken fern, coupled with full foliage on trees and shrubs, provides lots of protection, making clean shots an impossibility. Small wonder that some veteran grouse hunters in Minnesota, Wisconsin, and Michigan won't set foot in the woods until October 1, when frosty nights fire the hardwoods and allow bird scent to linger.

When you do find September grouse, though, multiple flushes from still intact family units are possible. Sometimes, it is a simple matter to follow up scattered birds to get reflushes. But as a general rule, you will earn every bird you pocket.

By mid-October, after the first freeze or two, dying bracken turns brown and wilts and trees become barren of leaves. The fall shuffle—that annual dispersal of young-of-the-year grouse to breeding territories—is in full swing, and birds again may be well scattered (though still usually found in the habi-

Ruffed grouse love edge cover; when leaves are still on the trees, hunting edges like these affords more open shots.

tats described earlier). Most of the hunter harvest occurs from mid-October until mid-November.

The best place to find December grouse is in what I call "green stuff," pockets of evergreen cover such as cedar or spruce swamps, pine plantations, and the like. Find green stuff that abuts mature aspen or birch clumps, and you will probably find grouse. Why? The conifers provide cover from weather and predators, and the aspens offer buds, the birds' main winter fare. On only one occasion have I found December birds in food cover—a combination of sumac and gray dogwood tangles that rode a half-mile slope—without security cover, such as evergreens, nearby. It is likely that these grouse had flown a half-mile from a pine shelterbelt at the back of the farm we were hunting.

When hunting in snow, look for tracks because grouse often walk surprisingly long distances in their search for food. This is especially true on warmer winter days. On bitter cold ones, the birds seem more inclined to fly to feeding areas. I have followed their triple-toed prints for up to a half-mile before wing prints in the snow showed they took to the air. Sometimes, you will find

When snow arrives, grouse move into more secure cover such as pines and other conifers.

several oval depressions in the snow where grouse roosted. Usually the depressions contain green-yellow droppings.

In deep fluff grouse often burrow completely under the insulating snow, which keeps them both warm and safe from predators. When snow is nonexistent or too crusted for their use, we have found them roosting in conifers. These cloaking covers offer a good place to hunt in early morning or late in the day. Peak winter hunting times, however, are midmorning through late afternoon when grouse can be caught in either food or security habitat or en route to one or the other. Two other excellent times to go are just before and just after a winter storm because hungry birds will be on the move.

Snow and cold weather, along with a shrinking dinner table, tend to concentrate grouse, too, sometimes in bunches of a dozen or so birds. It is not uncommon to walk for hours without luck, then suddenly hear the roar of wings from a half-dozen birds that you might never see.

Another good idea, either during the regular or late season, is to watch for that first snowfall. First snow gives grouse a false sense of security, and they will often sit tightly like fall-flight woodcock. This behavior offers excellent opportunity for nose-sticking work from your dog.

FIND THE FOOD NICHES

Even in poor hunting years, there always seem to be pockets of grouse. To find them, think small. Begin with the food factor: Although grouse will eat nearly anything, they often favor one type over others. I think of a certain stand of old apple trees where birds always go when the fruit begins to blush. Grouse also love late-ripening blackberries, shaggy manes, and other fall mushrooms, wild currant, and frost-puckered grapes with their high sugar content. These foods tend to grow in small places and are easier to target than, say, rose hips or wintergreen berries, which can be ubiquitous at times. A writer friend of mine who specializes in deer hunting calls this phenomenon the "least factor." So if you know where such favored foods grow in limitation, go there.

The food niches may be as small as a single tree. I remember bowhunting for deer one afternoon from a tree stand. Nearby lay a big aspen, freshly toppled by a storm. About an hour before dark, four grouse suddenly descended upon the aspen to rip away at the thousands of fresh buds. Easy pickings for them. Easy pickings for me. Next morning I traded the bow for my 28-gauge and shot two birds.

When the gunning is sweet and grouse seem to be everywhere, I grow a bit sad. I feel sorry for the naive grouse that got caught too far from escape cover or that held too long for my setter. That bird goes into the game bag with the other easy ones and the growing number of shotshell hulls that rattle together. But for every good grouse year, I can remember a half-dozen so-so seasons and one or two where the birds were so scarce I wondered why I bothered to buy a hunting license. Then I think about my favorite hunting companion (my dog) and how good the decaying woods smell and how wonderful it feels to be in shape after a summer of sloth, and I know why.

This grouse taken in Nova Scotia was feeding on fallen apples.

THE GROUSE CYCLE

Populations of ruffed grouse in the upper Great Lakes region tend to cycle in 10- to 20-year-long periods. Theories abound as to why. Some believe numbers are linked to predator abundance or scarcity. For years others have pointed out changes in habitat, food availability, weather, and even hunting pressure. A more recent argument blames a digestive system parasite that spreads when birds contact each other. The healthy ones survive and the parasite all but dies out until grouse numbers rise again. Grouse hunters in New England, Pennsylvania, and New York also experience population swings, perhaps for this or other reasons.

Last fall was a good grouse year in Michigan. Friends and I flushed 137 birds during the three days of our annual bird hunting camp in the Upper Peninsula. The closest we've come to that figure in the past decade was a mere 69 flushes in 1991. That was also the year we moved 185 woodcock, which is still a record. One afternoon last October, while hunting a favorite downstate grouse covert, a buddy, his son, and I flushed 23 different grouse (I don't count reflushes) in a little over two hours. There were so many birds that they were out of prime habitat. My dog pointed one in a weedy ditch, 20 yards from the woods. Another, boring right at me, nearly dusted my hat with her wing feathers. I killed both "gift" birds.

But how do you score when the cycle is at its low ebb, and gift grouse have all but disappeared? My advice: go bowhunting, take up bridge, or sharpen your bird-hunting skills.

When grouse are reduced to the population's backbone, those left are more than lucky. They are hardcore survivors that have been successful in dodging winged and land-based predators, both four-legged and two-legged types. The problem with ruffed grouse is that they rarely act like we expect them to. Even in years of relative abundance, they are

The author (kneeling) and his friends map hunting plans in Michigan's Upper Peninsula.

hardly easy to take. From the lushly verdant hell of September, through the skeletal aspens of late October, and into the cloaked conifers of winter, grouse maintain the upper hand, even for those hunters with the best of dogs.

Today's grouse remind me of arrogant cock pheasants—those artful dodgers with pin-drop hearing and 500-watt bulb brains—that know when to skulk, when to hide, when to run, and when to fly. A couple of anecdotes will illustrate just how elusive grouse are.

One December day two of three birds I flushed burst to freedom after making sure I had walked past them. Both times my dog was casting upwind and didn't smell them. I marked down the grouse in the "heard but not seen" column of my notebook. A hunting partner off to my left about a hundred yards must have spooked the third bird. Spotting movement through the hardwoods, I watched the grouse glide by on silent wings and suddenly drop into cover about a city block in front of me. Moments later Fagin, a setter I owned at the time, locked up on the bird. When I couldn't produce a flush, I released the dog, who tracked the running grouse a hundred yards and then slammed into a point.

"This time I've got him," I thought to myself, noting a clearing not 20 feet in front of the bird. "He's got to flush and if I can get to the opening first, he's mine." I was two steps from a clear shot when thunderous wings broke the spell between dog and bird. I missed, twice, in a scene right out of a David Maass painting.

How can I forget it—the gray-phase bird bursting through the ghostly birches in a machine-gun blur; the dog standing at attention, head up, wondering why I missed; the warm light of winter striking the inch of new snow, which sparkled like tiny jewels. Every grouse hunter experiences spectacles like that, and they serve to endear us more deeply to the bird.

That grouse ran the length of a football field. Not unusual, you say. What about a grouse that sprints three times that distance? One day two of the nine grouse a friend and I flushed turned into long-distance runners. His Brittany and my setter took turns pointing a grouse that streaked first through pole-sized aspen and then into a sea of conifers. He ignited into flight on the other side of the evergreens. Spotting him briefly, my friend saluted the bird with a snap shot. "Hope he's around to breed next spring," he said.

An hour later I was strolling through scrub oak, my 28-gauge at port arms, my dog casting off to the right. A sudden whir of wings to my left spun me around, and I missed a grouse exiting not 10 feet from where I had just walked.

"Did you see him?" I asked my partner. Before he could answer, a second bird flushed and dodged its way to safety through the oaks and my shot pattern.

"No," my partner said. "But there could be another." There was, but I was fumbling for shells when it went up. I marked the bird, called in the dog, and we decided to follow him up.

Macbeth, another setter I owned and loved, struck a point well over 100 yards away where the grouse had touched down in mature woods devoid of understory and holding little ground cover. "I'm sure he'll run," I said, which proved to be the day's understatement. That bird led my dog and us through the woodlot, across a logging road, and through another patch of woods. I'll be conservative and say the distance was 300 yards; for all I know, it might have been a quarter-mile.

I whoaed Macbeth again and again, until we exhausted hunters could catch up. Eventually, I began to lose confidence in my dog, who occasionally tracked rabbits and once had a problem with chasing deer. Macbeth's final point was 50 yards away. She looked over her shoulder at me as if to say, "Don't you want this bird, Tom? We've come this far!" The dog broke on her

Hunting close to a good dog greatly improves the odds of bagging a ruffed grouse.

own, tracked another 10 yards, and *bbbbrrrrr,* the bird detonated and sailed over a ridge.

Another time I was helping a game biologist track a grouse through radio telemetry keyed to a tiny transmitter the bird wore around her neck. During an hour-long stalk we flushed her four times; on one occasion she ran 250 yards between flushes. We saw her once.

To harvest such smart birds, you must trust your partner and stay up with him. When hunting any kind of gamebird, the dog is always the middleman. Pulled ahead by the racing bird, the dog must be constantly controlled by the hunter because dogs that race ahead and bust birds, regardless of whether the breed is a pointer or flusher, are of no help to the hunter.

Dog and hunter are a team and unless you learn to work together, you're in for a long, fruitless day in the woods. When you're up against a quarry like today's ruffed grouse, you need all the teamwork you can get. Who would guess that grouse, which in unhunted areas have been known to sit on a limb and wait to be shot, could be so savvy?

Other tactics involve tips I have explained more fully elsewhere. These include cutting off escape routes, anticipating and then forcing the flush, knowing your gun, hunting comfortably, and always expecting a bird to be smarter than you are.

For many upland gunners, autumn and ruffed grouse are the highlight of the hunting year.

CHAPTER
6

The Ring-Necked Pheasant

Have you eaten a pheasant drumstick lately? If not, you may be surprised at how rubbery and tough they are, the result of generations of breeding running genes. Man has tried, mostly without success, to fully domesticate wild pheasants for more than 2,000 years. Left to their own devices, while being hunted throughout the land, they just grow smarter and smarter. The fat, corn-fed pheasant of the nation's farms is no pushover these days, and prairie ringnecks—those stealthy, savvy birds that use their brains to dodge coyotes, hawks, and owls—are even tougher. Even with vast holdings of Conservation Reserve Program (CRP) land, there isn't much cover on the grazelands and native grasslands of Kansas, Nebraska, the Dakotas, eastern Montana, and even portions of Iowa, Missouri, and Oklahoma.

In the 35 states with hunting seasons, pheasants that learn how to hide and dodge and skulk and know when to run and when to fly survive to breed again.

So it's back to school for hunters who want to score on these new-breed

In spite of 2,000 years of attempts at domesticating the ring-necked pheasant, the bird has retained much of its wild character.

birds. The first lesson is understanding how well pheasants know their home territories. What appears to be a monoculture of grass, broken here and there by coulees and hills, contains a lot of hiding places for a smart old rooster with spurs like golf tees. I have seen pheasants flatten out in cover so thin you wonder how they could possibly hide their brightly painted faces.

HUNT THE SMALL PLACES

I have never shot a ringneck from a chisel-plowed field. But I have taken birds from patches of brush and woods, overgrown fencerows bordering farm fields, and strips of weeds that the center-pivot irrigation rig missed. In the East, many of these small places exist in both rural and suburban areas.

Keep an eye out for "pocket" covers like these as well as abandoned railroad rights-of-way, livestock watering ponds, shelterbelts, unkempt orchards, weed-plugged roadside ditches, abandoned farms, stream-bottom woods, and especially those wonderful CRP fields in their third year or later of set-aside.

If the cover you are sizing up and thinking about hunting all looks alike, look again. Pheasants often seek out micro-habitat within the larger scheme. A plum thicket in the middle of the prairie, for example, could hold all the birds you'll need today. A slight change in elevation, which creates a seam of heavier, lowland cover is another example. A little piece of head-high foxtail, perhaps a corner where the plow missed, could produce the only ringneck in a 40-acre field. An experienced dog always checks out these spots of micro-habitat, and you should too.

This Kansas CRP field of big bluestem is a haven for pheasants.

HUNT QUIETLY

A second key to rooster tails sticking from your game bag is understanding how well pheasants hear. I once read that a ringneck can detect the sound of a cannon shot at a distance of 350 miles. Who would know? Still, before you pouch the next rooster you bag, take a minute to separate the tuft of feathers covering the bird's ears. You might be surprised. If we hunters had ears of comparable size, the openings would be as round as teacups. Pheasants hear far better than most hunters realize. Being as quiet as possible will turn the odds in your favor.

HUNT THE HEAVY COVER

As crops are harvested and freezing temperatures strip the trees of leaves and turn the vegetation rank, pheasants become more vulnerable. These factors, plus hunting pressure, dictate how the birds use habitat that appears to shrink day by day. Pheasants are well-equipped to survive the elements, especially if they can find habitats that are more and more secure. As the pheasant becomes increasingly vulnerable to all forms of predation, he turns to the toughest, nastiest protection he can find. The deeper into the season, the deeper into impenetrable cover he goes.

We speak of the ringneck as an upland bird, but he becomes a lowland creature—seeking cattail pods, giant ragweed sloughs, wild cane stands, marshes containing phragmites, and other thick, safe cover where the tractor cannot go, the hunter doesn't want to go, and the snowstorm has little effect.

This ditch full of ragweed is the only pheasant cover available now that all the crops are in the elevator.

Ask any duck hunter where he sees and hears roosters in the late season. Then, expect to get wet.

Some ringnecks spend all fall and winter on wet ground, venturing out to feed on grain missed or spilled by the combine, roosting among dry cattail pods, even swimming to the safety of muskrat houses when pursued. To hunt these savvy birds, you'll need a pair of hip boots or chest waders. Tips: (1) Arrive before daylight and try to pinpoint roosters by their calls. (2) Use a fresh tracking snow to advantage. (3) Hunt slowly and as quietly as possible because surprise is your best ally, and most ringnecks will sidestep or double back rather than flat-out run off as many do in farm fields. (4) Bring a buddy, though, because big marshes can be a death trap in winter if you fall through the ice and are alone.

HUNT ALONE OR IN SMALL GROUPS

Pinning down running pheasants and forcing a flush is easiest to do when the habitat is linear, such as a fencerow or a few rows of uncut corn or cane. It is hardest to achieve when the cover is sprawling and can't be broken down into pieces. The multi-man pheasant drive originated in the big native landscapes and mile-long crop fields of the Midwest and Great Plains and, to some degree, it is still effective today. String enough people across the prairie, making sure the wing walkers are a bit ahead of the main drive and that there are blockers waiting at the end, and you'll kill some ringnecks.

But you'll bag far more birds if you hunt alone or in the quiet company of one or two others and, especially, if you seek out the smaller covers within the larger habitat.

Pheasants that sense danger—and this may be most of the time during hunting season—nearly always head for available cover. Shelterbelts, abandoned railways gone to seed, riparian cover, and field corners missed by the plow or center-pivot irrigation rig are all good places to look. Some of the best hunting I have enjoyed in Kansas, Nebraska, and both North and South Dakota has occurred while posting or driving shelterbelts. Pheasants roost in the thickest shelterbelts around, they ride out storms in their protection, and they sprint there for cover when threatened.

HUNT THE ROOST

Roost hunting is one of the most effective ways to bag ringnecks if your state's daily shooting hours start early and end late. On cold days birds often stay in the roost well after sunup and enter again by early afternoon. On the other

A close-hunting shorthair helped corral this CRP ringneck.

hand, storms, either present or impending, will keep them in the feeding fields for longer hours. The key to hunting a roost is to approach quietly from the downwind side to avoid spooking birds, which usually sit tightly rather than run off. A close-working dog, preferably one that checks back for hand signals, which precludes the need for a whistle or shouted commands, is a bonus.

In North Dakota a couple of Decembers ago, friends and I were able to catch ringnecks late in the roost one frigid morning. However, we shot very few from the cloud of 50 or so that exited because a high wind put the birds on edge and the main drive began before blockers arrived at their posts. I'm convinced those pheasants heard the flank hunters moving into position. How do I know? Because they ran up an unposted slough and flushed low from the other end about three times beyond shooting range.

Another trick we use to hunt prairie pheasants is to track them whenever there is snow. Hens, in particular, sit tightly in deep snow, and their silent presence while hunters crunch about and wheezing dogs cast for scent is sometimes enough incentive for nearby ringnecks to hold their ground. A further tip is to glass the edges of heavy cover during warm afternoons. A sunny day tends to bring pheasants out of the cover where they will lounge about in the tentative warmth. A good pair of field binoculars can help you to spot such loafing birds.

HUNT THE LATE SEASONS

Most bird hunters ignore the late seasons (in Kansas only 12 percent of the hunting pressure occurs during January, the last month of the three-month season), but don't be among those eager to rack their shotguns for the year. Access to private land is easier to get, especially with deer hunting seasons over. Bare fields and winter weather have forced birds into smaller pockets of cover. This scenario, along with the flocking instincts of pheasants, concentrates survivors into larger groups. But how late? Only three states end their pheasant hunting seasons in November. Fifteen others close sometime in December, thirteen more in January, and four states end in February.

CASH IN ON CRP LANDS

What I call Create and Reap Pheasants, the federal government terms the Conservation Reserve Program or CRP. Begun in 1985, the program at various times has enrolled more than 40 million acres of set-aside farmland throughout the country. Many of these cropless lands are blanketed with weeds; others support native grasses like big bluestem, Indiangrass, and switchgrass. These fields are easy to identify: Look for the thickest, heaviest cover around. Besides producing food and cover for songbirds and other nongame species, some CRP lands provide excellent habitat for pheasants, quail, Hungarian partridge, and plains grouse.

Some states, like South Dakota, have 2 million or more acres enrolled, but because CRP acres are privately owned, hunters must seek permission to enter.

Scouting in the area you plan to hunt should turn up plenty of these properties and offers the chance to look them over for hunting potential. Some are huge, a square mile or larger, and tough to hunt unless you have a small army of drivers and blockers. Choose those covers that appear birdy and can be handled by your group.

Most CRP lands are posted, and the federal Privacy Act means they don't have to be publicized. To find out who owns them, knock on doors or spend time at the county seat of government

A hunter and his Brittany are about to enjoy the fruits of hunting CRP land.

poring over plat books and scouring local telephone directories for addresses and phone numbers of absentee owners. Of course, it's always best to make an inquiry in person, but you can also do some detective work at home. Local chambers of commerce, Farm Bureau offices or county offices of the National Resources Conservation Service (NRCS, formerly known as ASCS) often know who has CRP lands, including those who welcome hunters for free or fee access.

DRIVES THAT WORK

Perhaps more than any other upland species, pheasants, those great runners of the gamebird world, lend themselves to the organized drive. One or more hunters walk the available cover with a plan, always driving birds to corners or fingers of habitat where other hunters, called blockers, seal off the escape routes and wait patiently. Just like a full-court press where the object is to force a turnover, pheasant drives force a flush. When pheasants have nowhere to go, they go up, giving both drivers and blockers chances to score. Five key considerations:

1. Drivers must work together to cover all the habitat. They should vary their cadence, stopping and starting, zigging and zagging, but always in the same line with each other.
2. Blockers must be absolutely quiet and stay put.
3. All hunters should wear fluorescent orange clothing, even in states where it isn't required.
4. In long, linear cover, it sometimes pays to have a flanker move downwind at least 50 yards off to the side in adjacent cover and 50 to 100 yards in front of the drivers. The flanker often gets shots at birds that erupt before running to the end where the blockers are waiting.
5. Groups of all sizes can make successful drives. Larger parties need a drive captain to size up habitat, make a plan, and then pair fast walkers together.

Here's a plan for a three-man drive: (1) in long, linear cover, one man drives, one flanks, and one blocks; (2) in rectangular or square cover, one drives a zig-zag pattern to pressure birds into the corners where two blockers wait.

CHINESE CHECKERS

Hunting pheasants is a lot like playing checkers because figuring out your opponent's next move is half the game plan for defeating him. Proper positioning is always the key, and in the game of pheasant hunting, out of position

The multi-man pheasant drive can be effective in big covers. A drive captain must size up the habitat and organize the hunt.

usually means out of luck. The days when ringnecks flushed beyond range for one hunter only to fly dumbly into another's are over. As one savvy hunter put it to me, "Roosters always know where they are going long before they take to the air. They know their home coverts better than any hunter, and they always know where the men and dogs are."

What can a hunter do, besides keeping as quiet as possible, to turn the odds in his favor? Here are four tips, all of which shake down to positioning:

1. Think ahead: Try to figure out where a rooster is likely to flush, then place yourself in the most advantageous spot. For example, whether or not you hunt with a dog, try to work into the wind whenever possible. Concentrating on what lies ahead will help you to identify fingers of escape cover, bottlenecks where you might pinch a bird into flight, and small hiding spots within the larger cover. Two hunters who know the habitat can work effectively on mini-drives—one walking and one flanking or posting—to put birds into the air. Likely setups for two-man drives include grassy terraces built to reduce erosion; fencerows and other strip cover such as standing row crops, grass-filled ditches, and hedgerows; brush islands in the middle of cultivated fields; river bottom tangles; rights-of-way along abandoned railways; stream bank thickets; and pockets of cover missed by chisel plows and center-pivot irrigation rigs.

The first part of good positioning is guessing where and when the flush will occur. The other half is choosing a good shooting lane. Don't stop, for example, in front of a wall of cover. Instead, either stop short or step around the obstruction. Many times I have bagged roosters that flushed on the far side of screening cover by running ahead or by merely stepping left or right for a clearer view. I shot back-to-back birds in Michigan last fall with this tactic. One ringneck exploded on the opposite side of a sumac-choked fencerow. By stepping into a tiny opening, I was able to cut him off with a load of copper-plated sixes. I killed the second bird by dodging around a wall of willow leaves that he intentionally tried to put between us.

2. Hunt hungry: The sharpest cockbirds allow only a second or two for a shot. That is why I don't tote my shotgun over the shoulder or in the crook of my arm. Instead, I always hunt with the gun at a 45-degree angle from the belt position and place my thumb on the safety and index finger along the trigger guard. A friend of mine, who hunts with a double barrel and is a better shot than I am, explains this stance as "looking over the muzzles" when anticipating a flush. Another tip I picked up from him is the step-and-slide method where the hunter approaches a dog's point by stepping forward with one leg and then sliding the other toward it. Try it; you'll never be off balance when a bird erupts in your face.

3. Watch your dog at all times: Knowing that pheasants nearly always flush in the same line of travel as a flushing dog, and usually in the same direction that a pointer is facing, will help prepare you for the shot. Staying on top of the dog, without pressuring it to work too quickly and thus mis-

These hunters teamed up with a good pointer to roust a ringneck into flight.

sing skulking roosters, is also good advice. Some hunters won't put their pointing breeds on pheasants because of the run-and-gun tactics necessary to get birds off the ground. True, it takes a special setter or pointer to handle pheasants with any success at all, and only a phenomenal dog knows when to stop and when to go.

4. Use hand signals: Talking with your hands to motion a partner into position, is better than hollering at him. When two hunters talk, a rooster quickly figures out how to avoid each of them. You can make a good dog better by training it to respond to hand signals, too.

One of the best all-around pheasant flushers is the springer spaniel.

Positioning grows in importance as seasons wind down. Although harvesting activities and killing frosts reduce available cover, surviving birds are more wary and tougher than ever to approach. Hunting late-season pheasants is a lot like selling magazines door to door: You have to knock on a lot of them before finding anyone home. On the other hand, when one is home, all are home.

Teaching a pheasant hunter how to position himself for better shots is a tough, if not impossible, job. You learn it by walking through hundreds of covers and remembering how birds act in each of them. In time, those experiences form a pool of wisdom in the memory that you will recall when faced with a similar situation. Whenever a rooster outmaneuvers me—then flushes out of range with a maddening cackle—I ask two questions: (1) Why did that bird flush from point A and not point B (or C or D)? (2) How could I have sized up the cover better and sealed off the escape route, thus forcing the bird to flush from a spot to my advantage? After 40 years I'm still learning how to play Chinese checkers. That's why it is so much fun.

HUNTING IN BAD WEATHER

You can take advantage of adverse weather conditions to fill your game bag with pheasants. High wind, for example, makes pheasants nervous because they can't hear danger approaching. If you work into the wind and are careful

These Iowa hunters teamed up during a snowstorm.

not to make noise, you can sometimes jump birds at close range. Wear woolen trousers or bibs that have been washed many times and are soft. Eliminate the clatter of shells in your coat pocket. Use hand signals to communicate with your friends, and refrain from blowing the dog whistle.

Rain is another tough-weather condition because cocks are hard to distinguish from hens, especially when water droplets spatter your shooting glasses. But if your dog hunts close and is under your control, you can actually turn a wet, sloppy day into a favorable one. Gone is the scrape, scrape of trousers across dry weeds, enabling you to get closer to pheasants. Also, birds are more reluctant to fly in the rain; as a result they skulk, double back, and try to slink away. A methodical dog will find them. A couple of years ago, we opened the season in a driving rainstorm. While stitching an invisible seam in front of two friends and me, Sherlock, my setter, abruptly struck a classic point, and then relaxed. Realizing the bird had already left, I released my dog, who then began a stealthy stalk—a rolling point, actually—for the next 15 minutes through the weed stubble. A hundred yards later, he nailed the bird cold. I looked in the tangled grass at my feet and spotted his barred tail feather nearly touching my boot. What had begun as frustration ended almost too easily.

HUNT ALL YEAR

I know that pheasant hunting used to be spectacular in many midwestern states like Illinois, Indiana, and Ohio, and many eastern states like Pennsylvania, New York, and even New Jersey. There are still birds and you can find them. Begin in late winter and early spring when the gaudy cocks are easier to spot, thanks to monochromatic covers beaten down by winter storms. Sparked by longer hours of daylight, roosters begin to move out from wintering habitat to claim breeding territories. Also, they begin to crow at this time of year.

Years ago I responded to an ad in one of the sporting magazines and invested in a Walker Game Ear. I now have two—one for each ear. These devices are incredible, so sensitive you can hear a refrigerator door open from the other end of the house and a ringneck pheasant crow from a mile or more away. Any loud noise, like a shotgun blast, automatically shuts down the Game Ear, before hearing damage can occur. Until I bought a second unit, though, I had trouble triangulating the exact location of sounds. Now, it is not unusual for me to hear one to five ringnecks crowing at a single stop.

From mid-March through early June, I drive along rural roads within 50 miles of my home, stopping along farm fields and brushlands with openings, and listen for crowing ringnecks (and the occasional singing bobwhite male). My setter and shorthair keep me company, by turn, in the pickup cab. I mark all crows on county maps, then revisit the site once or twice more to be sure the rooster has stayed put.

DEVELOP CONTACTS

I am always on the lookout for information about pheasants, and that is why I develop good relations with people in the know. The local game biologist, the county extension agent, the Farm Bureau contact, the guy at the grain elevator, the driver of the milk tanker truck, or the county road commission grader are all people who can share details about pheasant broods and who owns the hayfield next to the creek bottom and what his attitude toward hunters is. My UPS driver leaves packages with penciled notes scribbled across the top: "Tom—saw 8 chicks on Emerson Rd. a quarter mile east of Crenshaw." He gets a magazine subscription each year. Use your imagination to enlist other courier delivery people and every rural mail carrier you chance upon.

A young hunter's first pheasant. Who is more proud—dad or son?

Pheasant hunting is hard work. Dakota gunners take a lunch break.

CHAPTER
7

The Bobwhite Quail

I n the Western Hemisphere, the story of quail evolution is largely a southern phenomenon—that's why North America is home to only six species
(the bobwhite and five western relatives). There are nine additional
species in Central America and 15 more in South America.

Bobwhite quail follow mourning doves as the second most-popular gamebird (in terms of harvest statistics) in America. Bobwhites are the classic
gamebird—holding well for pointing breeds, offering excellent midday hunting opportunities, and challenging targets for young and old alike. A century
or more ago, someone characterized the bobwhite as a "gentleman's gamebird," and the moniker is still some-
what true today. The bobwhite is
revered wherever he is found, but in
the South, where quail hunting has its
roots, respect for "the bird" approaches
deification.

Today the bobwhite is legally hunted
in some three dozen states, thanks to its
broad range across southern and middle
America and to trap-and-transfer programs by state game departments in
other regions. It lives throughout the
eastern U.S. and is found as far west as
eastern New Mexico and Colorado and
extreme southeastern South Dakota.
Home range extends to southern New

*Range of the bobwhite quail has ex-
panded thanks to trap-and-transfer programs by state game agencies.*

England and southern Michigan, Wisconsin, and Minnesota. Winters are sim-

ply too punishing for its survival in Montana, North Dakota, upper regions of the Great Lakes states, and northern New England. Even in temperate Kansas an inch of ice atop a foot of snow can all but wipe out a local population.

Yet Kansas often leads the nation in the number of bobwhites harvested by hunters. I seek them often in the Sunflower State, as well as in Texas and Oklahoma, and I have hunted them in Missouri, Iowa, Illinois, Nebraska, Michigan, Georgia, North Carolina, and Tennessee at different times.

HUNTING TACTICS

One of the reasons I so respect the bobwhite is the bird's furtive nature. How a covey of 15 quail can hide practically underfoot—without movement or sound—is remarkable. Wizards at escaping, today's bobwhite will also run to cover, ducking behind thorny walls of multiflora rose, disappearing in a tawny sea of broomsedge, running out of range of the gun, and then flushing. One time I watched a male escape into a gopher hole. Thank heaven these birds leave scent for the dogs. A dogless hunter could stroll through prime quail cover and never see a bobwhite. I know because it has happened to me.

Quail are among our most gregarious upland quarry. They know that safety and survival are the result of togetherness, and that is why a bird separated from its covey is in trouble. Bobwhites roost on the ground in a circle with tails pointing to the center and heads to the outside. This arrangement provides warmth

Shooting only covey rises is as good as bobwhite hunting gets. This action occurred in South Texas.

on cold winter nights and instant flight to all compass points if the covey is threatened. Like pheasants and grouse, quail depend on the element of surprise to escape their enemies, and the collective roar of beating wings is enough to unnerve the steadiest of predators, especially those of us who walk upright.

Some hunters, blessed with an abundance of birds on the property they manage or have access to, shoot only the covey rises. Most of us, though, learn to mark birds where they land. Bobwhites don't fly very far—a couple hundred yards at best—and you can walk them up as singles if you know where they put down.

You can also listen for their calls. Sometimes in the morning the males will sing out and the hens will peep. The birds also become more vocal in late afternoon, as feeding individuals start thinking about covey security for the night. If temperatures are expected to drop below forty degrees, however, you should stop hunting an hour or more before sundown to give birds a chance to regroup. On a bitter winter night, a bird left out of the covey will be dead by morning.

SIZING UP THE COVER

The key to putting bobwhites in the game bag is to identify the habitats quail prefer, then learning when and how to hunt the covers effectively. Anywhere two types of habitat come together to form an edge is the place to start looking. Examples are weedy fencerows next to crop fields and corners of growth

This plum thicket in the middle of shortgrass prairie is a prime example of "pocket cover."

where center-pivot irrigation rigs, plows, and combines can't go. Weedy thickets, the fringe of a cattail marsh, sloughs containing brush or woods, un-grazed pastures, and ditches stuffed with weeds are other good places. If the cover is large, look for quail among the edges within—a crabapple thicket in an expanse of broom sedge, for example, or a seam of weeds in a field of cut corn or soybeans. Many times it is these "pocket covers" that hold the only covey in a 100-acre field.

TIMING THE HUNT

Bobwhites are creatures of habit. They like to roost in grassy spots with a southern exposure and often will form their rosette-shaped covey at the base of an osage orange, persimmon, or other singular tree, clump of brush, small patch of grass, or foxtail. Native grass fields such as big bluestem, switch-grass, Indiangrass, and cordgrass are attractive roosting spots. So are roadside ditches containing brome, broomsedge fields, or the edges of alfalfa plantings. Hunt these roosting habitats early or late in the day.

Quail eat a wide variety of weed seeds, grains, legumes, forbs, and nuts. In the Midwest, they like milo, soybeans, corn, sunflower seeds, acorns, and other mast. Southwestern foods include deervetch, thistles, and filaree. In the South bobwhites rely on beggar lice, lespedeza, chickweed, and partridge pea. In south Texas they eat the legumes, too, like snout bean and hoary and milk pea. If you can find these foods in close proximity to roosting and escape cover, you can probably find quail. Hunt the food sources in mid-morning and again in mid-afternoon. On frigid days, though, know that bobwhites typically feed around the clock.

Loafing cover includes broomsedge, prairie grass, meadows, mown or-chards, harvested fields of grain or alfalfa, and pastures containing some grass. Bobwhites use such habitats to preen, delouse themselves, and bask in the sun. The covers should provide some protection from the weather and predators. Hunt them at any time, but midday is best.

Escape cover is any of the above habitats that give quail an extra measure of protection. In areas where pressure from hunting or natural predators is high, escape cover figures more importantly. A screening canopy of ragweed, multi-flora rose, or heavy brush helps protect quail from hawks and owls. Wooded creek bottoms, junipers, and other evergreen trees and bushes afford shelter when danger approaches at ground level. Such vegetation also provides an umbrella of sorts when the skies send rain or snow.

In south Texas the birds use seacoast little bluestem, brown seed paspalum, and balsam scale for protection. I once hunted in Missouri for three straight days during a cold, freezing rain in November. Nearly all the coveys we flushed were from such screening covers in close proximity to food. Understanding how and when the birds use available cover is the best strategy.

THE MIDWEST IS BEST

The Midwest is the best region to hunt quail in America. There, I said it. And the best hunting comes from a handful of states that straddle the Corn Belt where the soil is so rich it can grow 150-bushel corn and 50-bushel wheat and where—when the winters are mild—bobwhites breed themselves into enormous coveys and the hunting is like a handout from heaven. Kansas, Iowa, Nebraska, Missouri, and Illinois are the best states. Yes, add Oklahoma, too, although you might rightly argue that it belongs to the Southwest and not the Midwest.

When you come to the Midwest, you'll want to bunk over in a place like the Heartland Motel in Ames, Iowa, where you can wear fluorescent orange to the local restaurant and not receive the kind of stares people give sideshow freaks. After tramping slough bottoms all day, you'll want to order one of those giant corn-fed beefsteaks—so big there is always a generous piece left for your hunting dog back in the truck. A whirlpool is nice for sore legs at day's end. Some Midwestern motels actually cater to hunters by providing kennels out back for bird dogs and a warm corner of the basement to dress birds.

The Midwest usually leads the nation in annual bobwhite harvest. This hunter moves in on a point on a CRP pasture in Kansas.

Late in the season you can knock on farm doors and, hat in hand, get permission to hunt especially if you are alone and invite the farmer to go with you and, if he can't, offer to bring him a few dressed birds. Midwestern hospitality is legendary. One time in Kansas, I asked eight landowners for permission to hunt and got on seven farms. The fellow who turned me down had promised his son and some college buddies that he would save the farm for them.

He felt so bad because I had driven a thousand miles from home that he offered to call a neighbor and put in a good word for me.

If you're coming for the season opener, however, you will not get on private land but will have to settle for public areas that are managed for quail and other wildlife. Some of these are very good on opening day, and they improve again in the late season when the crops are harvested and quail foods and covers have shrunk. Then, the birds move back onto the public areas.

Many native Midwesterners don't bother to hunt quail until the ground freezes and snow begins to accumulate. Coveys are easier to find then, especially if hunters wait an hour or two after sunup to give birds a chance to move around and scatter scent for the dogs. From midmorning on, we nearly always find bobwhites foraging in picked grainfields, weed fields, or pastures. The coveys typically spread out in an area the size of a football field but—as mentioned earlier—are usually only a short jump away from woods, brushy fencerows, or other escape cover.

A new setter pup I introduced to quail in Kansas years ago stuck a couple birds from a feeding covey. I killed a cockbird, which the five-month-old pup partially retrieved. It is for glorious moments like this that I love to hunt quail with pointing breeds, but I also know sportsmen who prefer springer spaniels, Labradors, and other retrievers that flush. They seem to enjoy the game as much as I do.

While hunting in the Midwest, things easily lead on to other things. A few snowflakes riding a cold morning wind down from the Rockies can make a man think about chili for lunch. At sundown the covey-up calls of bobwhites lead to a cock pheasant crowing to a barred owl hooting to a deer snorting from a field edge. Game is not as

This young hunter shot her birds at midmorning on a cold day in Kansas.

isolated as it is in the West, and it is nearly always more abundant than in the East. Thus, a rabbit scooting down a cornrow may lead to a fox squirrel chewing you out from an oak limb. Below the branch a covey of bobwhites could be diving for cover in a blackberry thicket.

Late one November some friends and I stayed at an old clapboard farmhouse near Memphis, Missouri. Our plan was to hunt 3,500 acres of ground leased by another friend, George Euson. "How many coveys on the place?" I asked host George at supper.

"The landowner figures about 100," George said.

One hundred coveys? Was it possible? That night, buried under quilts in the unheated upstairs bedroom, I could hardly sleep, wondering what the day would bring. I like staying in old farmhouses, like to be in a place where the floorboards creak and a pup can piddle on the floor and no one gets too worried. All night long I wondered if other generations of quail hunters had also listened to the wind whistle around the eaves of the old place and how the hunting would go the next day.

It went well, thanks to good dog work from Pete, Euson's seven-year-old pointer, and the fact that 1,200 acres of that leased ground was in CRP. We moved 14 coveys, more birds than I had ever seen in one day with the exception of South Texas. We found some of the quail in foxtail near fencelines of scrub oak and osage orange. We jumped other coveys from draws where locust beans littered the ground like giant black curley cues.

And we bumped birds from alfalfa field edges where the gooseberries were frost-puckered and the round hay bales looked like tired rolls of shredded wheat. Across the road, at a safe distance, Amish schoolchildren played at recess.

You can hunt quail in other parts of the Midwest, too. Southern Michigan, Indiana, and Ohio come to mind, but bobwhite numbers are never very high in these states due mostly to habitat fragmentation and the fact that they are too northerly.

Good quail cover in Nebraska is prairie grass along a river bottom with standing timber.

THE SOUTH IS STILL GOOD

I have had the opportunity to hunt wild birds in the South where writers like Nash Buckingham and Archibald Rutledge made Mr. Bob the stuff of legends. Unless you have an uncle who is a peanut farmer, the sport (for wild birds, anyway) is frightfully expensive. A few elite landowners, mostly in Georgia, still manage for wild bobwhites, but nearly every commercial operation has to supplement—at best—with liberated quail. At worst, they have few if any wild quail left to manage.

This situation will not improve appreciably, if at all, in spite of major efforts by Quail Unlimited. Gone are the small family farms that made up the rural South after the Civil War. Pine is now king in many areas once devoted to crops, and landowners who do manage for game are often more interested in growing big-racked whitetails. Prescribed burning, so important to the rejuvenation of native grasses and quail foods, is on the wane. Not so the march of predators—migrating hawks and owls from the north, raccoons, opossums, and armadillos from everywhere it seems. Nearly everything from snakes to fire ants loves to eat quail eggs.

Although wild bird shooting is still available in the South, it is getting harder to find for the average sportsman who punches a time clock and carries lunch in a bucket. That is not to say you can't journey and hunt private land for wild quail. Some public hunting grounds are managed for bobwhite production; however, the better ones require a little homework to find. If they get listed in an outdoor magazine, they will probably be burned off before you find them. Knocking on doors is a possibility but not a very productive one. Southern landowners fiercely protect their birds.

One suggestion is to telephone (or better yet, inquire in person) district wildlife biologists or public hunting lands managers for local information. Another is to buy an ad in a newspa-

English pointers are the preferred quail dog in the South where bobwhite hunting has its roots.

per offering reciprocity ("I'll show you grouse or pheasants or ducks if you show me quail"). A third is to book a hunt with a shooting preserve for liberated quail and then hope you stumble into a wild covey or two. I have done this successfully near Marietta, Georgia, at Burnt Pine Plantation, in southwestern Georgia at Pine Hill Plantation, and near Pantego, North Carolina, at Pungo Acres Hunting Retreat.

TEXAS—LAND OF THE BIG COVEYS

Texas is the land of extremes. Maybe it's the state's sheer size—wildlife researchers recognize 10 different ecological regions. Maybe it's just, well, Texas. I mean, there is the rest of the country and then there's Texas. Stepping off a plane one July afternoon at Dallas/Fort Worth Airport, I was greeted with a blast furnace of 104-degree temperature. When I went back the following January to hunt quail, naturally I forgot to pack gloves, and so I shivered in a winter rain even though I was hunting quail only a stone's throw—by Texas standards anyway—from Mexico.

They say the soil in Jasper County in east Texas was so poor during the Depression that if you planted two seeds, one would push the other out of the ground. Along the coast, a farmer could lose 50,000 acres per year to sand dunes. Why? Because the winds that roar through Corpus Christi are stronger than those that blast Chicago. You hear a lot of stories like that in Texas. Some of them are true.

I have learned three things during several visits to the Lone Star State: (1) venom from a diamondback rattlesnake can take the paint off a pickup truck, (2) it is wise to ignore those little red bottles of sauce you find in restaurants featuring home cooking, and (3) bobwhite numbers can rise and fall faster than the Dow Jones Industrial Average after a bulletin from the Federal Reserve.

It is the bobwhites that keep bringing me back to Texas, where I have experienced the best quail hunting days of my life. But, true to her occasional schizophrenia, Texas can be as stingy as an old crone with a sour apple for a heart. Yes, bobwhite hunting can be a boom or bust affair.

The hunt of all hunts for me occurred in the late 1980s when two friends and I rented a van in Dallas and drove 10 hours south to hunt on a private ranch between Corpus Christi and Brownsville. South Texas is not the land of milk and honey, though. It is the land of beef, brush, and bobwhites and is unlike anyplace else I have ever hunted for upland game. Sweeping grazelands that run horizon to horizon are broken here and there by oak mottes and clumps of mesquite, which the locals say was imported from Mexico. And there are more booby traps for walkup hunters: catclaw, wait-a-minute bush, and tasajillo or jumping cactus. Bright green mistletoe winds its parasitic vines around stunted oaks. Snakes pose a constant threat during warm weather.

We were hunting on a former preserve that hadn't been gunned since the Eisenhower administration. Our guide was 75-year-old Bill Weeks, who at the time trained and owned nearly 100 dogs.

"How do you think we'll do?" I asked from the backseat of Bill's hunting truck. Turtle like, Weeks turned completely around to look at me, his Stetson brushing the truck roof liner. "We'll do just fine," he said. "You are in south Texas now."

We drove for several miles through country as flat as pear juice on a plate. "Stop here," Bill finally said to his Mexican driver. "This looks as good as anywhere."

After booting three dogs, our guide tossed a pinch of talcum powder in the air to test the wind. Then he let go the charges. Speck, a five-year-old male setter, headed for the cover like a white rocket. Babe, an 18-month-old pointer, was close behind. Running circles around the truck was Sausage, a three-year-old springer spaniel used for close-up work and retrieves. A friend of Bill's joined the three of us hunters in the pickup. We racked our unloaded guns in holders and leaned elbows over the truck cab to watch our guide direct the dogs with whistle and hand signals from his scoop seat mounted to the front bumper.

Bill hollered "Point," before the truck had bounced 100 yards. But Speck's ramrod tail was lying, and so we hunters unloaded our guns again and climbed back into the rig. Twice again this happened before the setter stuck a live covey. Snaking low, Babe slid to within 20 yards, then backed in stretched tension, like an elastic band.

"Go git 'em," said our guide.

I took the left side and my shooting partner claimed the right. Twenty birds rose in a brown-and-white clatter, and my heart jumped into my throat. The targets seemed so little after an autumn of swinging on bomber ruffed grouse and fighter-plane pheasants. Five bobwhites tumbled before our guns. "I've got the flyers marked," I told Bill after Sausage had dutifully returned the final bird.

"Naw, let 'em go. We'll find another covey soon enough."

When rainfall is plentiful, Texas becomes known as the land of the big coveys.

We did, too. Fifteen more coveys and three hours later, we ended the hunt. *So this was quail hunting, Texas style?* I remember thinking. *Sixteen coveys for three hours?*

The next day was better. We routed 15 coveys in the morning and then 9 more during a rain-shortened afternoon hunt: 24 coveys for 5 hours.

"Is this as good as it gets or what?" I asked Weeks.

"No," he said. "My best day ever was 40 covey rises."

While I write this, I can still hear the creak of the truck and the swishing of Sausage's stub tail against my hunting trousers as we jounced along.

What is now called the Pineywoods of east Texas was the best quail habitat in the state prior to land-use changes that began after World War II. Today, the highest numbers of birds occur in south Texas and in the western half of the state, excluding the panhandle, which is home to mostly scaled quail. There is also decent hunting in the Grand Prairie region of central Texas where creeks with dry feeder streams fringed with thickets, low bushes, vines, and trees finger out into the grasslands. Over 100 years of continuous livestock grazing in this western region brought about an invasion of the prairies with brush and lower successional grasses and forbs to provide bobwhites with cover and food.

PEN-REARED VERSUS WILD QUAIL

Can you tell a pen-reared bobwhite quail from his wild cousin? I can. Liberated birds don't run as far and are not as hair-trigger nervous on the rise, preferring to flush underfoot rather than on the edge of range. When they do take to the air, there is a decided difference in speed, adroitness at dodging trees, and putting brush between you and them. Game farm birds often smell of captivity; sometimes they taste like the processed food they eat.

So, why hunt them? Well, do you want a few bobs bouncing around in your game bag or not? Yes, I hunt pen-raised quail and am happy to report that modern methods of selective breeding, rearing of birds in big flight pens, and early release to the wild is making it more and more difficult to tell the wild bobwhites from the liberated ones. Managers know the prescription to turn around the continued decline of wild birds, but it is expensive and time-consuming. And it often runs counter to conflicting land-use interests from farmers, ranchers, and land developers.

Good or bad, I see a big future for pen-reared bobwhite quail.

Careful management helped these pen-reared bobwhite quail to fly almost as well as wild birds do.

Bobwhites are the ideal bird to train a young dog. This Labrador retriever obviously likes the taste of feathers.

CHAPTER
8

The Woodcock

I do not remember the first woodcock I ever shot. The first ring-necked pheasant was different. Who could forget that brightly painted head, kaleidoscopic breast feathers of copper and purple and green, and bayonet tail with 32 bar markings? But a goofy-looking six-ounce bird with buckskin-colored breast, insect eyes, and an ice pick for a bill? No, woodcock number one didn't go into the brain file. But each one registers now and so I turn them over and over, check the legs for bands, and measure bill length with a dollar (the male's bill is under three inches, the hen's is slightly longer than three inches—the width of a dollar bill). I bury my nose in their breasts, trying to detect the faint odor of perfume and hoping to learn something about where they have been and what they know that I don't.

Yes, I've got it pretty bad for what many hunters call the timberdoodle, and over many years I've collected a game bag full of experience and memories afield. Maybe someday I'll remember the first one that found its way into the pouch.

Woodcock are, well, weird. They look as awkward in flight as a woman wrestler on a skateboard. It seems as though the whole bird is put together wrong. Insect eyes bulge from the top of the woodcock's head, and a duck has more tail feathers. My kids, now grown, used to say "Yuck. They taste like liver." A yellow Labrador, long-gone now, used to fetch everything from cow chips to the neighbor's garbage but refused to pick up a woodcock. Was it bad taste? Loose feathers? I never understood the reason.

Yet the 'doodle is my favorite upland target. How is it that a goofy-looking bird that weighs a scant six ounces can cause a man to kick his wife awake as he strolls through alder tangles in his sleep?

Here is why: No other gamebird sticks like flypaper for pointing dogs. Woodcock can humble the best wingshots when they meet the timberdoodle

Woodcock are the essence of autumn, and the forest uplander's great prize. These birds will hang for several days before being prepared as a delicacy.

on its own terms—bamboo-tight jungles of aspen and alder. Besides waterfowl and doves, what other migrant gamebird waxes strong as the season wanes? Is there another bird whose silent flight and secret comings and goings add more mystique to frost-fired autumn woods?

I don't think so. I used to snapshoot at the deceptive little targets, which zigzag away on soft, battering wings like giant brown moths, while hunting ruffed grouse. In those days, we considered woodcock to be incidental game—something we would shoot at but rarely hit. Over many years, though, I have grown to appreciate the bird's wily ways and, believe it or not, his excellent fare at table.

HUNT THE HABITAT

Like any other form of upland hunting, woodcock gunning is something you learn through time and experience. The most important thing to know is that habitat and timing are twin keys to a successful hunt. Most good shooting ground is in or near slashings or whips—those stands of young aspens—alder thickets, cattle-cropped pastures, abandoned orchards, marsh-edge uplands, or old fencerows. Damp, rich earth attracts feeding birds that probe for worms in the evening and throughout the night.

Resting areas, where woodcock spend daylight hours, may be traditional grouse habitat—aspen cover, witch hazel or hawthorn clumps, gray or red osier dogwood, sumac tangles, and even new conifers. Woodcock often get under the evergreens on rainy days. They prefer low-spreading junipers and other dense conifers such as balsam and hemlock, but we also jump them under pine and spruce trees.

The best cover will usually resemble a park of young trees, quite open at ground level (get on hands and knees for a look) with just enough canopy protection to give birds a sense of security from raptors. Woodcock like to be mobile on the ground, both to escape danger and to scout for earthworms,

Classic woodcock cover is a mixture of aspens and alder with moisture nearby. This habitat is in New Brunswick.

their favorite food. That is why you'll rarely find timberdoodles in grass. Bracken ferns, on the other hand, are okay since the birds can see and move through them.

Wet streaks of whitewash (woodcock excrement) that look like a sloppy painter splashed paint from a too-full pail are a dead giveaway that birds are available or that they just moved on. Find borings where they drilled for worms and you have a feeding zone for sure. Whitewash splashes alone spell out a brief resting area. If there are no worms, though, the birds will leave. During their migration, woodcock may consume a pound of earthworms (which are 85 percent water) every day, and they will eat around the clock. I have watched woodcock feed during the day, and I have shot a few birds that still clutched live worms in their bills upon retrieval by my dog.

THE MIGRATION FACTOR

Woodcock are either migrating or are ready to migrate when fat begins collecting along the sternum, over the lower back, and around the thighs. A research biologist, who is a hunter and a friend of mine, calculates that when fat deposits comprise 17 percent of a woodcock's overall body weight, the bird is a migrant or soon will be.

You've probably heard it said that woodcock are where you find them. To a degree that's true, especially during the October migration. We have shot them in open fields while pheasant hunting. Sometimes we've found them along edge cover a long way from water. One time we gunned them in pocket cover where the birds plunked down in the middle of a chisel-plowed field. Another time leafless sumac tangles crawling up the side of hills held the birds in stiff concentration. I'm not sure why; after all, the soil under that sumac was pure sand.

Such incidents are usually exceptions. A good tip to keep in mind is to hunt the bottomland cover during dry autumns. In wet years, work the upland areas. Remember that woodcock want both food and cover, and where you find one bird there will almost always be another. And another.

The best early-season gunning in the upper Great Lakes, southern Ontario and Quebec, the Maritime provinces, and New England occurs in young aspen stands that host an understructure of ground cover such as witch hazel. Here is where the birds rest and feed by day. At night they seek more open areas, such as old pastures and abandoned orchards. Early-season flush rates after the typical September open season in most states and provinces are excellent, although birds in the bag may be another matter. Why? Well, September is a green hell of foliage.

When low pressure systems combine with cold fronts, the aspen ground freezes, and that is when the real fun starts. Woodcock begin to stage in the last-to-freeze lowlands. Look for birds in balsam and spruce cover near alders or in areas of beaver activity. Although the longbills' general movement is southerly, there is plenty of east-west drifting as they travel in search of food. High nighttime winds with any kind of southern bent can postpone flights and stack up birds in tremendous concentrations, especially along rivers or roads, their primary travel corridors. These conditions produce the 100 flushes per day and the 1,000-bird evening flight stories we have all heard.

I've never seen such a migration, though, nor have I met a reliable eyewitness. The migrations, however, thought to be as long as 200 miles nightly, occur over a period of several days or weeks. Young-of-the-year woodcock and females are the first to go, replaced by birds flying in from the north. The adult males, smaller than adult females, leave last; so if you are still shooting hens, it is a safe bet that flight gunning is not yet over.

Migrants tend to move on cold, clear nights of a waxing moon. Dark, stormy nights and winds with a southern bent will hold them up, and if you know where to go, action can be too hot to handle. River valleys, tributary junctions, and even highways flanking good cover have produced for me. There is a place in Michigan's Upper Peninsula, for example, where a mile of mostly aspen woods connects two east-west running roads. Woodcock pile in here night after night until flight conditions are perfect. Get here on the third or fourth day of grounding weather (night conditions of high winds and low clouds with storms), and you will count woodcock in your sleep at the end of a perfect gunning day.

Migrant or local bird? There is no way to tell for sure, although fatty deposits on a bird's breast, thighs, and lower back are a clue the bird is ready to go (or is already on the move).

HUNTING BY THE CALENDAR

Many years ago I learned to hunt woodcock by the calendar. Based on my own harvest figures in Michigan, the best overall gunning occurs from October 1 to 15 in west-central counties of the Upper Peninsula for local birds (there are few, if any, flight birds that enter the region). Peak hunting in the eastern U.P. for mixed bags of local and Canadian flight birds occurs roughly during the same period up to a week later. The northern Lower Peninsula produces the state's highest harvest figures (along with the heaviest gunning pressure) with peak hunting from about October 10 to 20 most years. The best southern Michigan hunting occurs from about October 15 to 30.

Even so, I have shot woodcock until the Michigan season closure in early November and have seen birds while I hunted rabbits during Thanksgiving weekend. It all depends on the weather because a woodcock has no need to migrate as long as the unfrozen earth continues to produce invertebrates. The calendar, therefore, is far from absolute, but it is a guide—and sometimes a highly accurate one. October is the woodcock hunter's month, for those of us who live within 200 miles north or south of the 45th parallel of latitude. I base these observations on hunting experiences in Wisconsin, Minnesota, eastern Canada, Maine, New Hampshire, Vermont, and Massachusetts.

Although some woodcock occasionally find their way west of the Mississippi River, they are a gamebird of the eastern United States. Some birds reared in Nova Scotia, New Brunswick, Prince Edward Island, and New England move on through the Middle Atlantic states to winter in the Carolinas, Georgia, and Florida. Others follow the spine of the Appalachians into West Virginia and Tennessee en route to Alabama and Mississippi.

Woodcock raised in the Great Lakes region follow the Mississippi, Ohio, and other rivers—as well as superhighways and other roads—through Missouri, Arkansas, and on into Louisiana. Researchers estimate that up to 75 percent of the North American population overwinters in the Bayou State. Friends of mine successfully hunt woodcock in Missouri and Arkansas late in the fall, and I have shot them in Louisiana in January.

During a recent fall, a friend and I shot six woodcock that, I believe, were local birds in Roscommon County, Michigan. That occurred on October 13. On October 16, another friend and I drove 150 miles north and east to the

October is the woodcock hunter's month. A Maritimes tradition is to take a civilized lunch in the field. The author's wife and two friends enjoy themselves in New Brunswick.

eastern U.P. Here we enjoyed the best day of the season—35 productive points for our young setter. Yet the weekend before, another friend with a good dog flushed only one timberdoodle in this same cover.

As mentioned, woodcock remain in an area as long as earthworms and other protein-rich invertebrates are available. A dry fall will put 'cock on the migration wing early, while a wet one, with mild temperatures, causes them to linger. It is not uncommon for migrants to move in and out of the Deep South as temperatures and food availability dictate. I have heard returning males on the spring dancing grounds in Michigan as early as February 8 during a period of extended thawing in the north country. How can you not respect a bird that is so opportunistic and flexible?

Where you successfully hunted woodcock last year, you can expect to see them again, give or take a few days, the following year. Other than aspen, woodcock habitat changes little from year to year. No one harvests alder commercially, although the soil in mature stands of alder can become too acidic for earthworms to live. Find a good place for timberdoodles and you may enjoy good hunting for years.

This Louisiana hunter moves to edge cover where his pair of setters has located a woodcock.

The woodcock lives in a world of shadow and shine. The author's setter goes on point in a stand of moist-bottom alders.

FIREPOWER CONSIDERATIONS

Woodcock are not that difficult to hit once you learn how. Some hunters apply the simple "spray and pray" technique, which means fire at will once you identify the target. But this practice often cripples birds, and so I recommend picking your shots carefully. Use light loads (skeet or trap rounds are fine) in No. 8 or No. 9 shot. Skeet or improved cylinder barrels are ideal. These are fine, fragile birds that fall easily before a lightweight gun in 28- or 20-gauge. If there ever is a place for the underpowered .410 shotgun, it is in a covert full of close-flushing woodcock. Swing fast but don't try to follow the corkscrew flight of the bird. Instead, sight above him and fire as you and the bird reach the canopy. Woodcock have a tendency to hang momentarily before straightening out and resuming their escape through the cover. Most kills are made at this instant.

Woodcock are an absolute delicacy. Cooks who pitch out the little thighs with their lovely white meat or bake or broil the plump breasts to the consistency of boot leather should be palm-spanked with a spatula. For an incredible feast, marinate the thighs and boned-out breasts in your favorite recipe, then sauté them with mushrooms, onions, and garlic. I like to broil the marinated breasts on the grill, too, but only to medium rareness—the same way I like beefsteak.

Thick screening covers make for tight shooting. The best time to pull the trigger is when the bird reaches the canopy of cover where it will usually hesitate a moment.

A GAME OF HUNCHES

Hunches can be an upland gunner's best ally. Or so it was one October when my hunting partners wondered aloud if woodcock numbers were down. After all, three stops to once-productive coverts in northern Michigan had produced little in the way of battering wings and smoking shotshell hulls.

"Do you think the drought killed the young birds?" Tom, one of my friends, asked.

"I doubt it," I said. "They're probably in places we haven't looked."

So we tried elsewhere. Instead of aspen whips in the upland areas where the bracken fern was so dry that it crumbled underfoot, we turned to river-bottom cover. Here, under the alders, the ground was moist. I could still see my parked pickup through the just-turning trees when my little setter went on point. We shot that woodcock. Then, when the dog swapped ends to stick a second bird, we missed cleanly.

During the next 90 minutes, our group of four hunters flushed 24 woodcock, but the tight cover of broomstick aspen made for tough shooting conditions. We only killed four birds.

I'll take credit for having the right hunch about that little woodcock Shangri La along the river, but only because it was my idea to try other spots that earlier had failed. In truth, woodcock can pull disappearing acts that frustrate one as badly as an overdrawn checking account. Hunters have to adjust their hunches, and tactics, accordingly. To illustrate, I well remember another year when plenty of rain fell during our weeklong bird hunting camp in the Upper Peninsula. As the woods grew wetter, we found more and more woodcock returning to traditional coverts of aspen clearcuts.

In extremely dry years, though, woodcock tend to hug the lowland edges of such slashings. During wet years, look toward the highland centers of the clearcuts. Rainy days often send birds to individual conifers on the perimeter or within the slashings themselves. Like most hunters, woodcock hate to get wet.

We have also learned that when leaves begin to blush, curl, and fall—usually in early October—woodcock move from newer clearcuts to older ones. Then, our best gunning occurs in covers that are 5 to 10 years of age and 10 to 20 feet tall. Ground covers tend to be taller and more mature, but the same park-like openings mentioned earlier must be present. Keep an eye peeled for splashings, but remember that streaks resembling dried chalk mean birds have already gone.

A bonus of hunting the taller, older coverts is that they nearly always contain grouse. As the leaves go down, the canopy opens up and shooting scores improve.

The differences between lowlands and uplands may be very subtle—as little as 5 to 10 feet of topography. Unless you go afield with a knowledgable hunter, you may have problems identifying these differences. I remember hearing how a veteran New England grouse and woodcock hunter came to Michigan one fall but flushed very few birds because he was not accustomed to plunging into 200-acre aspen clearcuts. Nor did he have the experience to find the micro-habitats within the ocean of slashings. A small, damp area the size of a two-car garage may hold the only birds for acres. You have to see these places and experience them underfoot before they register as future possibilities.

Changes from habitat to habitat can be subtle, as suggested above, or highly dramatic. Just about the time I'm feeling smug over discovering a bird-rich cover, I'm mildly shocked to learn that

Don't fall into the habit of thinking woodcock are always in the same places. This hunter scored by moving into more mature cover comprised of mixed hardwoods and evergreens.

two days later (we never hunt the same coverts on consecutive days) the cupboard is unaccountably bare.

THE SECOND SEASON

Some of us who appreciate woodcock extend our "hunting" seasons to the spring when we listen and look for the male's mating dance and get involved with finding and banding broods of young birds. Although some woodcock breed in southern states, most of the continental population of several million birds begin life in the North. Every night, from March through May, the optimistic male woodcock puts on an aerial ballet, which is unmatched by any other bird in North America. The best time to hear and see the display is in that magical time between sundown and full darkness.

Choose an open area, such as an abandoned pasture, which is growing back to brush or young hardwoods, especially aspen. Quietly place yourself along the edge of the eastern side and listen for the buzz-like sound of the male. This unusual noise, which biologists call a "peent," sounds as though it might be coming from an insect and not a bird.

When the peents grow more rapid in succession, the bird is ready to launch. The instant the peents stop, he will take to the air in a spiral ascent that grows wider and wider until he reaches heights of about 300 feet. If you're lucky, you may spot the bird for a second or two as it rises. If you miss him, listen for a chirping sound from high above, then a twittering—the sound of wind rushing through wing feathers as the woodcock falls to earth.

If a female is available and if she approves of his exhibition, the pair will mate. Hens build a shallow nest in this same habitat of young-growth forest. Typical of snipe and certain other shorebirds, they lay four eggs, which will hatch in about 20 days.

As far as researchers know, woodcock raise only one brood per year. Strong renesters, in the event the eggs are destroyed by a predator, hens are very successful at rearing a high percentage of their precocious young to adulthood, perhaps more successful than any other upland gamebird. The young are capable of foraging for themselves at only a few hours old. Within a few days, they begin to fly. In the market hunting days, long before regulations, some woodcock gunners took to the woods as early as the Fourth of July.

THE IDEAL GAMEBIRD

Woodcock are the perfect gamebird for young dogs and young hunters. Apparently they exude a lot of scent, and they often hold beautifully, not like those long-legged pheasants that drive pointing breeds nuts. Like other upland species, though, the woodcock has learned that its legs may also carry it to safety. The fact that birds sometimes dash through an alder run or patch of aspens only to flush at the far end serves to endear the bird to me all the more. I like to hunt setters and pointers over woodcock, but flushing breeds will do the job, too. I know dogless hunters who are also successful at bagging woodcock, but, as you know by now, to my mind that is like going hunting with half your clothes on. I don't want to hunt birds without a dog.

Dogs have taught me much about themselves, about me, and about woodcock, whom I have observed looking at an unsteady setter in the eye at 18 inches and then, like a poltergeist, whisking itself away on thin air. I know no greater joy than hunting with a young dog in a covert stiff with flight birds.

First points, those puppy-clumsy, screech-to-a-halt antics that have the Brittany wrapped around itself like colors on a barbershop pole, are always special. I like the high head and buggy-whip tail of a proper pointer, a check mark frozen in time. I like to see any pointing dog's tail quiver and nostrils flare as the trance-like dog sucks up scent from a bird perched just off its nose. Sometimes when that happens and my mood is right, the dog's eyes aren't the only ones that water.

A Gordon setter proudly holds a woodcock. Is there a better bird for pointing dogs?

Where are the woodcock today? The author (right) discusses the possibilities with Jerry Dennis and Tom Carney, fellow writers and bird hunters.

CHAPTER
9

The Partridges

Partridge offer some of the finest wingshooting I know, and yet little is written about these great gamebirds that mostly live west of the Mississippi. The late George Bird Evans ignored them completely in his book, *The Upland Shooting Life*. Geoffrey Norman, author of *The Orvis Book of Upland Bird Shooting*, devotes just three paragraphs to the Hungarian partridge and only one to the chukar. I can think of only two writers who consistently contribute magazine articles and who have penned books extolling the merits of partridge. They are Ben O. Williams, who lives in Montana, and Charlie Waterman, my Floridian friend who has been chasing Huns for more than half a century.

There are three kinds of partridge in North America. The chukar is hunted in the high country of 10 western states. The range of the Hungarian is broader. It includes the prairie provinces, many western states, and extends into Minnesota and southern Ontario. The snowcock is fair game only in Nevada's Ruby Mountains. All are Old World birds, imported to North America over the past 100 years. Among the ornithologists who study evolution, there is general agreement that partridges, along with francolins and quails, belong to *Perdicini,* one of two tribes of the subfamily *Phasianinae* or Old World pheasants (the other tribe is *Phasianini,* which includes pheasants, jungle fowl, and peafowl).

Partridge are different from grouse, most conspicuously because they lack the feathered feet of grouse. Male partridge also differ from cock pheasants, which have spurs on their legs. *Vive la difference!*

THE CHUKAR

First introduced to the New World in 1893 by W. O. Blaisdell of Illinois, hundreds of thousands of chukars have since been released in 42 states, the

Chukar country is as tough as upland hunting can be. This scene is in northern Nevada.

Hawaiian islands, and several Canadian provinces. Most of the transplants, however, failed. Popular as a preserve bird throughout the country, you can hunt wild chukars in Nevada, Oregon, Washington, Colorado, Montana, Utah, Wyoming, Arizona, California, Idaho, and British Columbia. The best sport occurs in Nevada and Oregon where, in a good year, hunters will bag a quarter-million birds each.

There is no comparison between hunting preserve chukars and wild birds where enclosures are absent and the terrain is usually rugged. I read somewhere that a chukar hunter's downhill leg is longer because of the 45-degree slopes the birds often favor. Chukars may live as high as 10,000 feet. As night descends, they usually fly to lower altitudes to roost near each other under shrubs and rocks or in low grass. Roosting spots are nearly always on slopes with a southern bent, which are good places to begin a morning hunt. Chukars move up during the day, feeding as they travel, to take advantage of the sun-warmed rimrock and outcroppings where they lounge and survey their domain for danger. The birds can scurry under rocks when avian danger—hawks and eagles—approaches.

During the hunting season, chukars feed mostly on green matter and seeds such as filaree, watercrest, rough fiddleneck, smartweed, and cheatgrass. In farming areas, they will also eat corn, alfalfa, and orchard fruit. Because water is important, a good place to hunt is near man-installed guzzlers (there are more than 1,000 in Nevada alone). Late in the season, the lower one-third of elevations usually holds the most birds, which move progressively lower as the mountains fill with snow.

An Oregon Hunt for Chukars

The first time I hunted chukars was in north-central Oregon along the Deschutes River. Wind in late November plays games in hill country. One minute, there is not a breath of it, and the blackflies droning about your ears annoy your ability to hear. The next minute you top the crumbling ridge, and a northern blast stands your hat and tears your eyes. Gladly, I would have traded sweat droplets for tears. For two hours I had dragged my exhausted self across an enormous hillside of crumbling earth, trying to reach the top and certain sweet relief.

My right leg throbbed painfully, in harmony with the tiny tack hammers that rapped away at both temples. So this was chukar hunting? It reminded me of high school football practice many years ago when our coach, his crew-cut bristling and neck muscles bulging, forced us to run wind sprints up the local Heart Attack Hill.

But no coach had forced me up this hillside above the river that gleamed far below like a silver thread. I had made that decision myself. And my two hunting partners were worse off than I; after all, they had opted for higher ground above me in hopes of pushing a covey of chukars my way. That tactic, incidentally, often pays dividends because the birds tend to run uphill and nearly always fly downhill.

Pausing to catch my breath, I heard one of my friends shouting. "Heads up!" the voice roared out over the canyon and was repeated on the other side. Next, a shotgun boomed and I listened to its repetitions.

Suddenly, there they were—a knot of birds dressed in gray and brick red coming by me at Mach One. They looked like the Swiss Army jets I had once seen on maneuvers in the Alps. With no apparent effort the planes cut left, then right, and disappeared as quickly as they had arrived. I didn't take their picture then; now I was equally surprised, with no chance to shoulder my gun. I watched the chukars, making strange *whitoo-whitoo* sounds, quickly disappear against the rimrock of the surrounding hills.

I could now add a beating heart to the throbbing temples and leg.

At that moment I became hooked on hunting these gray ghosts of the rimrock. And I was quickly learning that the passive hunter—the fellow who dawdles along and lets his mind slip its moorings for a moment—will put nothing in his game bag. Settling down, I shot the only other chukar I saw during one of the toughest hunting days of my life. I am looking at that handsome mounted bird as I write this.

A Nevada Hunt

Everything is in the chukar's favor. His large feet and strong legs enable him to sprint uphill faster than you can run. Powerful wings allow him to fly long distances, most of it downhill and at warp speed. It is difficult to get close enough for flushing shots because the sharp-eyed birds travel in flocks of a dozen to 40 or more. And the environment in which chukars live—rimrock slides, mountain peaks and saddles, desert plateaus, sagebrush uplands seamed with cheatgrass—is open and the vegetation is low growing.

"You have to go after them," said Bill Gibson, my guide on a December hunt in Nevada's East Humboldt Mountains. "And you need to work together as a team with a hunting partner. A good dog is a must." I looked at Agate, Gibson's Texas-size Chesapeake Bay retriever, and realized the man was serious. Other evidence was the guide's painful limp from a turned ankle he had suffered on a recent chukar hunt and a huge hickey on his shotgun. "That gun broke my fall and saved my life," he explained.

I wondered what was in store for me that day.

We parked Bill's old Suburban at the base of a mud-colored foothill speckled with clumps of sagebrush. A half-mile away and a few hundred feet higher, a talus of rimrock hung on the mile-high mountainside. Following Agate, Gibson and I fanned out and started uphill.

Dogs do make a difference. Two minutes and 100 yards later, Agate bumped a covey of chukars into rattled flight. I pulled feathers on one bird and dropped a second, which the big dog gleefully returned. We topped that ridge, were swallowed momentarily by a valley, and began tackling the rise on the other side where four inches of snow remained from an earlier storm. A good sign, I figured, because snow sometimes helps to hold birds, that is, if chukars were like other gamebirds.

They were. Four suddenly rocketed out from a tangle of sage. I hit one and watched him flutter away into another clump of sage. Hearing wings behind me, I spun around and folded a single with my second barrel. Not a picture-perfect double perhaps but close enough to make me feel pretty good about my shooting and the Winchester one-ounce loads of 7½ shot I had slid into the 28-gauge. The period of self-congratulation was brief, however. The first bird I had dropped into the sage was still fluttering. Suddenly it took wing again and flew 100 yards before setting down.

Agate nailed that bird. A good dog is necessary because even in plateau areas where you can see for miles, the ground cover looks the same, and it is difficult to mark dropped birds. Further, chukars can absorb a surprising amount of punishment, and a hit bird may glide for hundreds of yards before piling up.

We began walking the contours of the hills, one hunter above the other, to pinch birds into flying. Bill bagged a couple of chukars I sent his way, and after missing some, I potted a single on a right-to-left swing just before it topped a hill.

That made 5 birds for 10 shots. My sixth (and limit) chukar required five more shells. That was another single, a low flusher, which I hit at 30 yards. Feathers exploded and hung on the air, but the bird kept going. Two hundred yards later we put him up from some cheatgrass, and I folded his tent for good.

What a fine day of bird hunting that was! The irony, of course, was that everything had been imported for the hunt. The chukars were introduced from Asia, the cheatgrass from the Russian steppes (where it hitchhiked in the wool of live sheep a century ago), the gun from Japan. But the sunset that sent us back to Elko was decidedly American, the alpenglow on the Ruby Mountains uniquely Nevadan. That night I slept like a baby.

THE HUNGARIAN PARTRIDGE

"The Hun has no tradition, glamour, or press agent—except me, and I don't work at it full time," Charlie Waterman was once quoted as saying. That's too bad because the little gray-and-rust birds, which fall between ruffed grouse and bobwhite quail in size, offer good hunting opportunities in South Dakota, North Dakota, Idaho, Montana, Oregon, Washington, Nevada, Utah, and Wyoming, along with Alberta, Saskatchewan, and Manitoba. In the Midwest, they may be hunted in Nebraska, Iowa, Wisconsin, Minnesota, Missouri, and Illinois. Limited opportunities exist in New York and southern Ontario and Quebec. In truth, a growing number of upland gunners are discovering their charm, to the extent that some areas now produce more Huns in the annual gamebird harvest than pheasants.

The earliest introduction of Hungarians, also called European gray partridge, I could find in my research occurred in Washington State in 1906. The descendants of birds released in Alberta two years later expanded into Saskatchewan, North Dakota, and Montana where they found cultivated lands, open terrain, and climate to their liking. Long ago in Hungary and Czechoslovakia, the partridge had adapted to people and their farming activities.

In North America, fall and winter survival is high except when affected by severe ice storms or deep snow. As is true with other upland species, dry, warm spring weather and the availability of insects determine whether chicks survive to be recruited into the general population. Land-use patterns that leave waste wheat, barley, oats, and other grains in the field and edge cover along fencelines, field borders, and shelterbelts are other keys to stable numbers of Huns. Living on weed seeds and other plants, gray partridge are also able to survive on the open

The Hungarian partridge is finally earning the respect it has long deserved among upland hunters. A Chesapeake Bay retriever fetched this North Dakota bird from a shelterbelt.

grasslands and prairie sage lands. However, they are harder to find there.

Hunting Tactics

Huns closely resemble bobwhites in their daily habits and habitat choices. Refer to that chapter for details about feeding, loafing, and roosting covers within habitat that offer security. An excellent time to hunt gray partridge is right after a snowstorm. Then, hunters often drive roads looking for the tracks of birds seeking grit.

Although I have hunted Huns successfully in Montana, Nevada, and both Dakotas, I have yet to experience what veterans tell me is a banner day—6 to 8 coveys numbering 12 to 20 birds each. Luck, I'm sure, has much to do with that. I canceled airline tickets to North Dakota one December when a blizzard blanketed the state and severely depressed what had been a burgeoning Hun population. Targets next fall were hard to find. Another time commitments precluded my going to Saskatchewan for what

Gray partridge resemble bobwhites in their daily habits. Here is evidence of a roost.

was promised as the "best Hun year in a decade." And just last fall—when numbers supposedly were high again in North Dakota—my best day afield was three coveys.

The nature of gray partridge is another factor at play here. I do not believe anyone can "promise" that Huns will do anything for certain or be found anywhere on cue. My experience says you'll walk a mile or more for every bird in the bag. Although most western farms and ranches have at least one "home covey," the birds are often not at home. Far less predictable than bobwhites or even pheasants, Huns may excite you into a lather when you see a covey of 30 birds feeding in the front yard of a farmstead—and into a funk when you can't find them the next day.

For this reason, many hunters think of partridge as a bonus bird, which they are all too happy to collect in pursuit of sharp-tailed grouse or pheasants. But I really like to hunt Huns on their own challenging merits. Edgy birds that typically flush for pointing breeds on the outer limit of range, they often ignite as a single rush of wings amid a cacophony of squeaky chatter. Gregarious almost to a fault, they find safety in numbers. Mark well their flight because birds often sit down as a group where they may (or may not, being Huns) hold better for the reflush. Huns don't fly as far as sharpies, and be-

Many upland gunners view the Hun as a bonus bird. These hunters collected a Hun and a sharptail while hunting the Badlands of North Dakota.

cause they are smaller are easily lost on the horizon. Short, strong wings carry those compact bodies to safety in a finger snap.

One time in Nevada, a friend and I bumped a covey of a dozen Huns. They flew off as a group, about 600 yards, before alighting at the mouth of a box canyon. Would you believe we put them aloft three more times before we managed to scratch down a single bird? We never did get closer than 30 yards. In North Dakota one time I knocked down a partridge at 66 yards with No. 7½ shot in the full-choke tube of my 28-gauge over-and-under. It was a foolishly long shot and I had to dispatch the bird, which was so beautiful that Dan Nelson, my hunting partner that day, had it mounted for me.

But shooting Huns is not *always* that tough. Last fall I returned to North Dakota and scored a perfect double with my new 28 side-by-side. The first flush caught two friends and me by surprise, and we either missed or were too stunned to shoot. We watched the birds disappear over a small rise in the wheat stubble a quarter-mile farther on. Topping the swell, I noticed a dark seam of weeds in the blonde stubble. "That's where they'll be," I predicted. And they were. I was in the middle when six birds went up, and I managed to drop the pair that swung over me at 25 yards.

If you are a hunter of Huns, you know how satisfying that was.

THE SNOWCOCK PARTRIDGE

To me, the ultimate upland gamebird is sometimes called the snow partridge, ram chukar, or snow pheasant. Its real name is the Himalayan snowcock (*Tetraogallus himalayensis*), and it is one of five species of snowcocks living in the high mountain ranges of central Asia. The Himalayan snowcock occupies the Kindu Kush, Karakoram, Himalayas, Pamir, and other ranges of Pakistan, Afghanistan, India, and China. In these places the birds live above 10,000 feet in winter; in summer shepherds and shikaris (local hunters) have seen them at altitudes nearing 20,000 feet. Some of those mountains climb another mile or more, and perhaps snowcocks live even higher. To elude human predators as well as eagles, vultures, jackals, and even the rare snow leopard, snow-cocks post sentinels and rely on keen eyesight and strong wings.

An overall gray-white in color, adult birds sport a snow-white mantle with sometimes a hint of light blue. Snowcocks blend perfectly with their Old World habitats and in Nevada's Ruby Mountains and are nearly impossible to see when they freeze in position. The sexes are similar except males are larger in size (about five pounds), have more black markings about the neck, and sport bumps where spurs would be expected.

The story of their introduction to North America is as fascinating as the bird it-self. In 1961 Reno sportsman Hamilton McCaughey traveled to the province of Hunza in Pakistan to hunt Marco Polo sheep. Enamored with the Himalayan snowcock, McCaughey obtained three pairs of captured birds and carried them by porter, pony, jeep, and airplane more than 8,500 miles to a quarantine station in Hawaii. Apparently needing grit, the snowcocks all but destroyed plastered walls in rest houses along McCaughey's travel route. Only one bird survived the month-long trek. Nevada Game Commission officials were so impressed with it, and McCaughey's zeal at introducing the species to portions of Nevada's 75,000 square miles of habitat devoid of gamebirds, that they decided to let him intercede on their behalf and obtain more stock from Pakistan for rearing at the state game farm.

The snowcock partridge is the second-largest North American gamebird (after the sage grouse).

A hunter glasses the peaks of Nevada's Ruby Mountains looking for a snowcock partridge. Note the Desert Storm camouflage he is wearing.

Between 1963 and 1979, biologists released 2,025 young in five locations, but only those releases in the Ruby-East Humboldt range were successful although the last time I checked there was evidence of a few birds remaining in the Toiyabe Mountains. Hunting seasons have occurred since 1981.

Glacial cirques are the key to snowcock survival in the Rubies, which is thought to contain 500 to 600 birds, or about one bird per square mile. Ringed by limber pine, the lovely cirques contain alpine meadows of corn lily and fireweed along with grasses, forbs, and sedges. Seeps flash in the sunlight. A pika resides on each incoming talus. The snowcock's habits resemble those of chukars except snowcocks apparently stay in the mountain peaks year-round. If you go, hunt them in September before winter snows seal shut the passes. Leave your dog at home—the rugged peaks are dangerous, and a dog would be a liability.

About 10 years ago seven of us, led by Elko guide Bill Gibson, rode horses to a spike camp at 9,500 feet in the Rubies. Each day for five days, we climbed to the rugged caprock at nearly 11,000 feet. Wearing Desert Storm or ASAT camo, we took turns posting outcroppings and driving mountain walls in hopes of sending panicked birds over each other. I lost eight pounds and blew out the sidewalls of a pair of sturdy Rocky boots, which I tossed into a dumpster in Elko after the hunt. I missed my only shot—a missile of a bird hurling across the vault of blue sky between peaks at 80 yards—with a round of 12-gauge No. 4 copper-plated shot. Two hunters in our group were lucky; each shot a handsome snowcock.

Yes, it was worth every ounce of sweat.

Bill Gibson, a guide from Elko, leads a pack string and hunters to the high country in quest of the snowcock partridge.

CHAPTER
10

The Plains Grouse

L ike other types of grouse, the plains or prairie species have feathered feet but differ from their forest-loving cousins in that they are flocking birds that prefer wide-open habitats. There are three kinds of plains grouse: sage grouse, sharp-tailed grouse, and pinnated grouse or prairie chickens. Sage grouse occupy specialized habitats among western rangelands and may be hunted in nine states. Ten states plus the prairie provinces of Canada host hunting seasons for sharptails. Greater prairie chickens may be hunted in Kansas, Nebraska, South Dakota, and Oklahoma. Limited hunting opportunities for lesser prairie chickens occur in southwest Kansas and the Texas panhandle.

Plains grouse are fun to hunt with or without dogs. Challenging to take on the wing, these dark-fleshed birds are excellent table fare. Whenever I travel west of the Mississippi River, I think about hunting them, and often do.

THE SAGE GROUSE

At three to six pounds, the sage grouse or sage hen is the largest of North American grouse. Males are nearly twice again as large as females and may weigh close to seven pounds. Both sexes have narrow, pointed tails and gray-brown bodies. The upper throats of adult males are black, the best way to sex them from females other than body size. They also fly differently: males struggle a bit to get off the ground and fly horizontal to it; females get up more quickly and dip left and right in flight. Sage grouse habits and habitats are somewhat similar to the other plains grouse except they occupy sagebrush, supplementing their year-round diet of sagebrush leaves with alfalfa greens and insects.

Nicknamed thunder chickens or bombers, the big birds have lived for so long on sage—one of the land's oldest plant communities—that they have no gizzard like the other grouse species. Sage grouse do not grind their food; a tough membranous lining helps digest their leafy meals.

The war on sagebrush by ranchers and farmers and the prolonged drought of the Dust Bowl years sent sage grouse populations to all-time lows by the Second World War. Most states closed their hunting seasons. Today the birds have rebounded well enough for seasons to reopen in several states. Wyoming, more than half of which is blanketed with sagebrush, leads the nation in harvest, followed by Idaho, Montana, Utah, and Nevada. Hunters take limited numbers of birds in Colorado, California, North Dakota, and Oregon.

I shot my first sage hen from rolling sagebrush rangelands west of Vail in Colorado. The juvenile bird looked like a grouse and flew like one. We ate it for supper that night, and, contrary to what I had been told, found it to be delicious. I have since shot them in Wyoming and Montana. I ate those birds, too. Field-dressing birds quickly can often improve taste.

One difficult part of bagging a sage grouse is getting close enough for a shot. Their long necks and propensity for gathering in flocks that may number several hundred birds make getting within shotgun range difficult. Also, strange as it seems, hitting a big bird

Sage grouse are never far from sage, their preferred food.

Because sage grouse are such large birds, you can often spot them with binoculars. Keep your dog in close, though, or they may flush before you can get into shooting range.

that appears to hang in the air can be a tall order. But sage grouse don't hover like sparrow hawks, and they can attain speeds to 60 mph.

Capable of flying miles in search of food, the birds rarely seem to be far from sagebrush. Good places to look for their feathers, droppings, and tracks are around stock ponds, watering tanks, and other sources of moisture such as irrigated fields and the damp bottoms of coulees and drainages. The grouse leave a lot of sign, especially when flocks number 20 or more birds.

Bring binoculars and get into the habit of glassing terrain. After a hard rain, you might spot birds sitting on humps or rocks to dry off in the wind. Early in the season before cold nights kill the grasshoppers and other insects, you can find sage grouse in alfalfa fields especially in the morning or afternoon. They like to loaf at midday in pockets of grass within the sage. Sometimes they roost there, especially if the grass has a southern exposure.

You'll wear down boot leather if you strike off across the sage flats in search of birds that may or may not be there. Ask ranchers, rural mailmen, and others who drive a lot if they have seen birds in their travels, then follow up with "when" and "where" questions. If you can pinpoint activity and location by time of day, you can return and hunt via one of two methods: (1) post a roosting or feeding site well ahead of the time you expect birds to return, (2) walk them up by heading into the wind. You may find it actually easier to get close to sage grouse without your dog because nervous birds probably will associate your four-footed partner with a hungry coyote.

One time while hunting north of the Musselshell River in south-central Montana, a friend and I took turns trying to drive sage grouse into an ambush. It worked for me when I hid behind a hay-bale round a half-mile up the draw from where midday birds were lounging. When my partner flushed them, some members from the flock of three dozen came right overhead, and I shot a big male. Unfortunately, the ruse didn't work an hour later when I tried to stalk the birds for my friend who was hiding in a small grove of cottonwoods. Just when you think sage grouse are predictable, they aren't.

These sage grouse hunters found success in Colorado.

THE SHARP-TAILED GROUSE

Adult sharptails are 16 to 18 inches long and weigh about two pounds each, the size of hen pheasants. A light underbelly and white dots on the wings add more white to the overall mottled look of both sexes. Chest feathers are punctuated with black chevrons. The tails of both male and female sharptails are squared on the ends. Central tail feathers on the male have parallel striping; on the females, they are mottled.

A popular target of hunters in Montana, Minnesota, and the Dakotas, sharptails are rarely hunted in interior Canada where they range from eastern James Bay to the Rockies and north into the Yukon and Northwest Territories on into central Alaska. Open seasons also occur in Wyoming, Colorado, Idaho, and Nebraska, and there are limited hunting opportunities in Wisconsin.

The plains race subspecies is plentiful from northern Alberta south through North Dakota. The prairie race lives throughout Manitoba, east-central Saskatchewan, western Ontario and the upper Great Lakes region. The Columbian subspecies is gone from Oregon, California, and Nevada—most remaining birds live in British Colum-

bia. Subspecies in the Northwest Territories, Alaska, and the northern prairie provinces continue to thrive.

At one time sharptails and prairie chickens were the same bird. Speciation occurred over millennia through flock isolation and the emergence of specialized habitats with the sharptail seeking wide-open plains and short-grass prairie, largely undisturbed and sprinkled here and there with brush. Home used to be most of the northern half of North America. The sharptail's range extended as far east as Illinois and as far south as western Oklahoma, northern New Mexico, and most of Utah and Colorado.

In most states sharptail hunting seasons open in September when young birds hold for the dogs. Protective cov-

Sharptails are abundant in several western states and provinces. The sexes are similar in appearance.

ers are densest then because the reduction process that begins with hard frosts and produces rank vegetation has yet to begin. I find family broods feeding in alfalfa fields on succulent leaves and tasty grasshoppers. In North Dakota, which usually has the largest number of sharptails and the best hunting, I also seek September birds in buffaloberries.

The buffaloberry or bullberry, as it is also called, is a bright red berry that grows in bushes from five to 10 feet tall. The plant thrives in coulees along the Missouri River, and in years when rainfall is adequate, the bushes appear to be on fire. Sharptails will spend Indian summer days alternately gorging themselves and loafing in these shaded grocery stores. A hunter can get unbelievably close for in-the-face flushes. Early last October while hunting a tributary of the Little Missouri River in western North Dakota, I was able to bag a three-bird limit within an hour. And I did it three days in a row.

Enjoy such moments because you will not likely get this close again. As fall passes into winter, sharpies group together in large flocks, and their keen eyesight protects them from predators in a world where security cover has grown lean. By December, a hunter is lucky to get within 100 yards of the high-strung birds.

The author shot this South Dakota sharptail with help from his shorthair, Boo. After ruffed grouse, the sharptail is his favorite grouse.

Late fall is the best time to post fields of milo, sunflowers, corn, winter wheat, and turnips because sharptails descend upon such favored fields in droves shortly after daylight and again at sundown. The trick is to choose a good ambush spot—hay bale, weedy fenceline, cattle feeder—and bushwhack birds as they fly on wings that alternately flap and glide.

Even in the late season, though, I prefer to walk up sharptails into the cold wind rather than waiting on the frozen prairie. I guess it's the joy of walking through the sweeps of grassland, unfettered by telephone lines and jet contrails. Anyway, I enlist the help of either a close-ranging Lab or a ground-gobbling pointer that knows enough to slam to a stop at the first whiff of bird scent. Sharptails invariably lie in the lee of hills

These sharptail hunters found success on the shortgrass prairie of North Dakota.

just over the crest. You often hear them airborne—their queer clucking sounds coming down the wind—before you actually see them. After ruffed grouse, sharptails are my favorite of the grouse gamebirds.

THE PRAIRIE CHICKEN

Some scientists believe the prairie chicken is the oldest grouse on the continent. At one time they lived in the midcontinent belt of lush, native tallgrass prairie from the eastern Great Plains through the upper and lower Midwest to Indiana and southwestern Michigan. Bits of tallgrass prairie reached into Ohio, Tennessee, and Kentucky, and small populations of chickens lived there, too. One early settler crossing the Appalachians found the birds to be as plentiful "as sands of the seashore."

Subspecies include the heath hen (an eastern bird extinct since 1932), the endangered Attwater prairie chicken (a few remain along the Texas coast), and the lesser and greater prairie chickens.

Once farmers plowed down grass-rich Iowa and Illinois, prairie chickens moved west with the plow. They found strongholds in Kansas, Texas, and

Oklahoma. The expansion, however, didn't last long because as settlers converted the prairie to rangeland or plowed to grow grain, the birds suffered. In places where the grass-to-cropland conversion exceeds 60 percent, chickens are virtually gone. Today, the world's largest remaining population of greater chickens lives in the Flint Hills of eastern Kansas. Besides the stronghold states, which host hunting seasons, small flocks are holding on in Illinois, Missouri, Wisconsin, North Dakota, Colorado, and Minnesota.

The greater prefers tallgrass prairie; the lesser lives in semiarid grasslands of shin-oak bluestem and sand-sage prairie. The lesser prairie chicken is about one-fourth smaller than the greater, which weighs about two pounds and tends to have an overall lighter appearance. Both sexes of both races have an upper plumage of barred brown and black feathers, and brown chest streaks across white- to buff-colored breasts. (In hand, these barred chest feathers make prairie chickens easily distinguishable from sharptails as the latter have a distinctive "V" pattern on chest feathers.) All chickens have feather tufts (pinnae) along the neck, but in males the pinnae are longer. The fan-shaped tail is short. In the cocks it is mostly black; in the hens it is heavily striped. Central tail feathers resemble a small brush dipped in white paint.

This chicken hunter shot a double in Kansas one January afternoon when a large flock came into the field to feed.

Like sage grouse and sharptails, the males sport air sacs, which inflate during spring mating rituals. The sacs are orange-colored in greaters and rose-colored in lessers.

Count yourself among the lucky if you find prairie chickens and sharptails in the same area. In both the sandhills of Nebraska and on the Fort Pierre National Grassland south and west of Pierre, South Dakota, I have experienced such banner days. In Nebraska, we flushed both species from an irrigated field of turnips. In South Dakota our group of nine hunters found scads of birds along a hillside during a September afternoon that was as good as modern plains grouse hunting can be.

I remember thinking that scene could be a page ripped from some market hunter's notebook. It might have occurred a century ago, and I fancied the creaking wheels of the wagons groaning behind our line of fire. Birds getting up—singles, doubles, and more—before the dogs, gunfire all along the hill, some grouse falling to the grass, others exploding to safety, only to lock wings and glide back to earth a half-mile farther on. We hunters moving on like a full-court press, the stream of birds rolling away before us like an endless covey, their chuckling sounds carrying on the breeze. The prairie light broken by shadow and shine as clouds scuttle overhead, the dancing grass like rolling waves in the distance. A land sculpted by time, warped by wind. Purple asters under my feet. The turpentine smell of gumweed on my pants. Nine limits: thirty-six grouse. A moment I wanted to last forever. Praise God for the Dakota grasslands.

It isn't always like this, of course. In years of drought, chickens and sharp-tails are scarce, and you can walk until your calves are tight as snare drums and never bust a covey. One year, for example, my friends and I coined a new name for prairie chickens. We called them the "six-for-one birds." You know: six miles for every flush.

THE FIREPOWER FACTOR

Plains grouse are a challenge to take on the wing. In the early season I choose 7½ shot in a field load and screw-in choke tubes of improved cylinder and modified. By late season, though, I switch to modified and full and want cop-per-plated 6s for two reasons: (1) the birds are better feathered, and, (2) they often flush at greater range.

Late-season prairie grouse hunters often have it all to themselves, and the soft, out-of-shape fellows who rack shotguns early say they are welcome to it. Sub-zero winds snatch body warmth. You'll need a woolen ski cap, insulated boots, and two handkerchiefs—one for tear-streaked eyes and one for a steadily weeping nose. Still, from late November through January (where hunting seasons are still open) there is no better time to let a prairie-bred wind straighten out the psyche, blow the funk from your soul.

Then, the best way to hunt plains grouse is to find a milo or sunflower field they are using and wait in ambush

Use enough gun in the late season because chickens and other plains grouse can be hard to kill. I like to use No. 6s in this 12-gauge L.L. Bean New Englander.

for them to sail in at first light or before dusk. We did that, several of us chicken hunters, in Kansas a couple of winters ago during a cold snap when snow on the hay bale rounds looked like cream over shredded wheat. We hid behind those bales and managed to shoot several chickens from a large flock. To successfully waylay prairie grouse, keep these thoughts in mind:

- Always take incoming or passing shots. Never shoot at a bird flying away unless you enjoy wasting ammunition.
- Plains grouse only appear to be flying slowly. Like Canada geese, they move much faster than they seem to. Also, like Canada geese, sharptails post a sentry bird.
- Use enough gun. Consider 12-gauge, No. 6 shot in a high brass shell.
- Movement distracts sage grouse, chickens, and sharptails, not sound. They have eyes like a pronghorn and run on their wings.
- Intelligent birds, they often grow wary if hunters rearrange a feeding field by adding blinds or moving landmarks.
- Typically, plains grouse feed in early morning and late afternoon. Cold weather brings them in as late as nine in the morning and as early as two in the afternoon.

As much as I enjoy pass shooting at plains grouse, I much prefer to walk them up, even in the late season when flocks may number a hundred hunter-shy birds. There must be wind, of course, but not too much wind, which waters the eyes and jeopardizes good shooting and which causes the dog to stand off from too far away. A gusting wind is also bad because it scatters scent and confuses the dogs.

A KANSAS EXPERIENCE

For two reasons I'll never forget Cawker City, Kansas. First, it's the home of the World's Largest Ball of Hay Baling Twine, something like eight tons and growing every year. Second, we were staying in Cawker, as it's known locally, when I shot as honest and clean a double on prairie chickens as I ever hoped for. That's a feat I'd been trying to accomplish for 25 years.

It happened, actually, closer to Hunter, another small town in Mitchell County in north-central Kansas. Last December our gang of 12 bird hunters got into the habit of dropping into the Hunter Café for the $4.50 lunch of fried chicken, mashed potatoes and gravy, corn, cole slaw, biscuits, and coffee with a generous slice of pie for another buck. I don't know how many people live in Hunter, but when I asked a local farmer, he put down his fork, shrugged and said, "I dunno, but I'm sure the population just doubled."

The hunt was organized for several outdoor writers by a group of manufacturers, and things were not going well. Bad weather, not enough private land to hunt, and a shortage of dogs conspired to do us in. If you had told me I would come to Kansas—that fabulous bird hunting state—for three days and not kill a pheasant or a quail, I would say, "Not possible." But that's what happened. In fairness, this was a late-season hunt, and the birds were edgy. Whenever our gang of drivers lined up in the prairie grass like a phalanx of orange fire, ringnecks flushed a half-mile away from the other side before the blockers were ready.

My first mistake was leaving my dogs home. The second was leaving my gun home. "Don't need 'em," our hosts insisted. "We'll be shooting Berettas." Now I know that Berettas are fine guns—they've been around for nearly 500 years—but these were automatics. Putting an unfamiliar shotgun, especially an autoloader, in my hands is like arming me with a bent two-by-four. I missed every one of the few shots I had. Autoloaders are fine for some, but I have no confidence in them; consequently, my shooting prowess goes AWOL.

Prairie chickens saved the hunt for several of us. One of our hosts had brought along a 12-gauge Beretta over-and-under and, when he noticed my tears, he loaned it to me. Armed with a pocketful of Impact loads, the new tungsten matrix shotshell from Kent Cartridge, I stuffed two No. 5 rounds into the chambers and took up a position along a fencerow. Chickens had been feeding in a winter wheat field here. Silent as a sneak attack of Japanese Zeros, they came in at 4:20 against a darkening sky. Friend and fellow writer Joe Arnette gave me the heads up. We arose together, he killed a bird and I painted through one chicken—killing him in the air—and took another the same way, as neat and as fast as that lunch pie had disappeared.

A good dog helps to find chickens on the walk-up and after birds fall on a posted hunt. This is a wire-haired pointer.

"I'm really glad you were here as a witness," I told Joe later, while he posed me for pictures. "But I sure wish I had my dogs along, and we could have walked them up."

CHAPTER 11

The Forest Grouse

It is no secret the ruffed grouse is North America's most popular grouse species. A bird of the forest and the forest edge, the ruff prefers mixed habitats of leaf-bearing and needle-bearing trees in settings with shrub understories and openings. Two other forest-loving species are the blue grouse and spruce grouse, whose specialized habitats often blend with or are next to the covers used by ruffed grouse. Most hunters either know little about them or dismiss them as unchallenging. They often call the blue and spruce species "fool's grouse" or "fool hens" because the birds act tame and appear stupid.

My experience is the opposite. Any grouse species—ruffs included—that do not see the gun tend to be unwary. In remote areas of Canada I have approached close enough to ruffed grouse drumming in spring or feeding in fall to almost touch them. In Alaska one time, a spruce grouse landed in a tree under which I was standing. The bird knew I was there and yet seemed unconcerned. I could have been another deer or moose. Another time in Nevada we were camped near a mountainside copse of aspen when blue grouse walked through our string of packhorses. They appeared to be curious, not afraid. I could have hit them with a rock.

Whenever I have hunted unsophisticated forest grouse with dogs, though, the birds act much differently. Feathered crests grow erect. Grouse amble off or tense for the flush. I assume they associate the dog with a coyote, bobcat, or other four-footed predator—danger signs no doubt encoded in their genes. So, as with all upland game, the dog makes a huge difference.

THE BLUE GROUSE

Sometimes called dusky grouse, hooters, mountain grouse, or blues, the blue grouse is a rather nondescript bird—an overall slate color with underwings of gray-white and a mottled chest of gray (males) or buff to dark brown (females). A little larger than ruffed grouse, the typical cock weighs two and a half pounds, the average hen two pounds or less. Biologists have identified eight subspecies.

They occupy coastal mountains from southeastern Alaska to northern California and live at altitudes from near sea level to several thousand feet. Interior races range from the southern Yukon and McKenzie River region through British Columbia and western Alberta into the northwestern states. Besides Canada and Alaska the best places to hunt them include the Cascade Mountains in Washington and the Sierra Nevadas of western Nevada and deep into California. Mountain ranges in southern Oregon, western Montana, and throughout Utah, Wyoming, and Colorado are also good places to go. More opportunities occur in some Arizona and New Mexico ranges.

I have hunted blues in Wyoming's Shirley Basin, in Colorado's Rocky Mountains at altitudes from 7,500 to 11,000 feet, and at 9,500 feet in Montana's Little Belt Mountains. Blue grouse are unusual in that they are reverse migrators—when most game leaves the high country, ahead of winter storms, for the lowlands, blues move up to timberline. Here they over-

winter while feeding on the buds, seeds, and needles of pine, spruce, fir, and other conifers. Besides food the evergreens provide security from predators and protection from deep snow and cold. In spring the males descend to open valleys containing mixed habitats of conifer, leaf-bearing trees, and shrubs—covers not unlike those favored by ruffed grouse. Females follow, then spend the summer working their way back up the mountain slopes, followed by their chicks.

Here is evidence that blue grouse are underharvested: during several hunting adventures with friends, we encountered only one other upland hunter. He was in the Helena National Forest near Townsend, Montana. He did not have a dog. He was carrying a .22 rifle, and his vest bulged with the weight of three

A Colorado hunter took this blue grouse, probably a migrant, in sagebrush flats, more than a mile from the nearest evergreen.

A Brittany returns a blue grouse taken in Montana. Dogs make all the difference when hunting unsophisticated forest grouse.

When blue grouse are the quarry, start hunting at timberline and then work your way downhill.

grouse. We had dogs and on that particular hunt shot several blues from the 20 or so we flushed. The birds were in classic blue grouse cover—small stands of treeline limber pine stitched here and there with aspens whose frost-fired leaves shimmered like gold coins. Except for one gawker that sat on a tree limb and stared at us, the grouse flushed well for our golden retriever and Brittany.

I enjoyed a terrific blue grouse hunt in Colorado one time, potting a true double (both birds in the air at once) from a small flock my yellow Labrador retriever and I surprised in a grove of alpine conifers just below timberline. I was hunting in the Vail Pass area at 11,000 feet. But blue grouse on the migratory move can be just about anywhere. Another time two friends and I shot nine Colorado birds from aspen patches in the middle of rolling sagebrush and rangeland. The altitude was 6,000 to 7,000 feet. Although I could see for miles, there was not an evergreen in sight.

The best way to find blue grouse during fall hunting seasons is to locate the types of habitat I have described and then hunt your way through them. Start at timberline and work your way along slopes and down their sides. Sooner or later you will encounter blues.

THE SPRUCE GROUSE

Perhaps even fewer upland hunters seek the spruce grouse, also called the black grouse or swamp grouse. Those after ruffed grouse or other gamebirds kill most of the 300,000 or so taken each year in North America. Like most blue grouse, the spruce grouse is not stupid, just unsophisticated. Few wingshooters venture into the climax conifer forest the bird calls home; consequently, few swamp grouse encounter two-legged predators and their dogs. A true wilderness bird, the spruce grouse also suffers less mortality than other grouse. One reason is the thick screening covers the bird calls home. The other is that spruce grouse don't concentrate like other grouse do.

Home is the northern boreal forest that spans the continent from coast to coast. Spruce grouse live throughout much of Alaska and in the spruce and larch boglands of the tundra region for hundreds of miles south into southern Canada and the northern United States. Three subspecies, respectively, occupy conifer forests through western Canada into the Pacific Northwest (the Franklin grouse), down through the Great Lakes region (the Canada race), and into the Maritimes and New England (the Hudsonian subspecies). A fourth group, the Valdez subspecies, lives in southern coastal Alaska.

This pair of spruce grouse came from Quebec's Far North.

Besides Canada and Alaska, the only places where you can legally hunt spruce grouse are in Washington, Montana, Idaho, and Minnesota. I have shot them in the Far North of Quebec near Schefferville, below the Brooks Range in Alaska, and in northwestern Montana. About the size of ruffed grouse, spruce grouse are likewise delicious. Like blue grouse, their flesh falls between light and dark—not as white as ruffed grouse but not as dark as plains grouse.

Michigan bird hunters I know have mistaken spruce grouse for ruffed grouse, accidentally killing what has been a protected bird for some 90 years. When lumberjacks cleared the virgin forests, they destroyed much of the spruce grouse's habitat. For this reason, hunting seasons were also closed in Maine, New York, Vermont, New Hampshire, and even in Nova Scotia. Thanks to modern management of our forest resources, they appear to be making a comeback in these and other places.

Adult males exhibit black throats and breasts of white and black feathers. Much darker in appearance than ruffed grouse, flashes of white are clues to their identification in flight, even in the gloomy confines of a cedar swamp. The birds weigh about two pounds each and are similar in size to a ruffed grouse. Spruce grouse hens and cocks typically exhibit a pale-orange band across their tail feathers. The slightly smaller hens are similar to female blue grouse except the spruce grouse hen has more white on its breast.

Spruce grouse live and die within a few acres of habitat if their life-cycle needs are met. Within openings and around edges of the brooding conifer forests are ground covers of fern and low-growing shrubs where the birds forage for typical grouse foods: blueberries, cranberries, whortleberries, crowberries, mushrooms, and various insects. By late summer, though, they begin to eat the needles of tamarack (larch), which turn color and fall to the ground like leaf-bearing trees. In winter their diet is entirely spruce, fir, and pine needles.

Spruce grouse appear to be making a comeback in several northern states. This one is a male (note the red eye comb).

Both sexes typically exhibit a pale orange band across the tail feathers.

This hunter scored from a spruce bog along the Dalton Highway in Alaska.

The best place to hunt them is along trails and tote roads and among edges and openings within the sea of conifers where they live. Flushes typically occur right in the face, and shots are close. If you miss, mark the bird carefully. It will not fly far, and you should have a second chance to shoot it.

THE CASE FOR MONTANA

Say "Montana" to a sportsman and his immediate associations are either fabled trout rivers like the Madison, Big Hole, and Clarks Fork or trophy big game hunting for goat, sheep, bear, mule deer, elk, lion, and antelope. Hardly anyone mentions the bird hunting. It, too, can be legendary.

Sharptails, sage, blue, spruce and ruffed grouse are available—all the species indigenous to the continent except for prairie chickens and ptarmigan—and if you are hunting in certain places and are lucky, you might even spot a protected white-tailed ptarmigan. And there are pheasants, Hungarian partridge, mourning doves, and even a few chukars in Big Sky country. Some upland gunners in the know come strictly for the sharptails or pheasants but are happy to collect bonus birds.

Montana appeals for so many reasons. First is the sheer enormity of the state. One afternoon a few years ago my family and I came down out of Glacier National Park where we had dawdled too long. Thus, it became necessary to put down the pedal on my pickup truck and make some miles. All night long we drove east on U.S. 2 and greeted dawn in North Dakota and said goodbye to Montana at—I think this is right—mile marker 674. Every time I travel to Montana I discover a new mountain range. People know about the Rockies, Absarokas, Beartooths, and Big Horns, but the Flathead, Bull, Judith, Highwood, Big and Little Snowy, and Little Belt mountains also beckon. Altogether, Montana is home to 56 mountain ranges.

The state is virtually empty, with about 800,000 inhabitants for its 145,000 square miles, which computes to about five people per square mile. The biggest city is Billings with only about 70,000 people. Helena, the state capital, is home to a mere 24,000 souls. Typical of the West, smaller settlements like Twodot and Sunburst and Pompey's Pillar and Checkerboard sputter and somehow stay alive.

Blue grouse are probably Montana's most underharvested gamebirds, although spruce grouse are also largely ignored. Many of the mountain slopes and valleys in the western region are home to blues. Statewide, the annual harvest is only 25,000 to 50,000 birds. Hunters take even fewer spruce grouse—5,000 to 15,000 most years.

In south-central Montana, blues and ruffed grouse are found in the Pryor Mountains as well as in the Beartooth Range and the Crazies. About two-thirds of the state's northwest region is in public ownership, and hunters will have no problem finding blue, spruce, and ruffed grouse in good numbers. The blue grouse is the most numerous gamebird in southwest Montana, and hunting opportunities abound on public land in the high country. Some sage grouse exist in high intermountain sagebrush communities, and a few spruce grouse are available as well as ruffed grouse that are localized near aspen stands at lower elevations.

CHAPTER 12

The Western Quails

When upland bird hunters think about quail, the bobwhite naturally comes to mind. But west of the Mississippi live five other North American species: the scaled, Gambel, valley, Mearns, and mountain quail. All are challenging gamebirds that are difficult to find at times and hard to pin down. That's because four of the five habitually run to safety. The other, the Mearns quail, is a shy, secretive little bird. The Mearns, too, will run when threatened, but it also freezes when danger approaches. This bird has nerves of steel; a hunter may step over one without causing it to flush. The five Western quail occupy specialized habitats, some of which, luckily, overlap because you may have to walk miles between flushes.

THE SCALED QUAIL

Scaled quail live in the Southwest although they have been introduced, with limited success, to other western states. Also called the blue quail and cottontop, the sexes are similar in appearance—blue-gray in color with a feathered, pointed crest a dusky gray color with a white peak, hence the moniker "cottontop." "Scaled" refers to the heavy scalloping of brown-tipped breast feathers that look like fish scales.

The birds prefer semiarid desert grasslands. Wherever I have found them—in the flat to gently rolling terrain of southwestern New Mexico, southeastern Arizona, southwestern Kansas, and western Texas—I have also identified certain vegetation: yucca, century plant, Mormon tea, Spanish bayonet, and various grasses such as tabosa, sacaton and side-oats grama.

Scaled quail are hunted in southwestern Kansas, southern New Mexico, south-central and southeastern Arizona, southeastern Colorado, Cimarron County, Oklahoma, as well as in the panhandle and southwestern regions of

Scaled quail are easily identified by their scalloped breast and neck feathers, which look almost like fish scales.

Oklahoma, and western Texas and the Texas Panhandle. Scattered populations live in Nevada, and they may be hunted in the Mexican states of Chihuahua, Coahila, Neuvo Leon, San Luis Potosi, and Zacatecas. The best hunting occurs in New Mexico where, in a good year, hunters will pouch 200,000 birds.

A "good year" occurs when adequate rainfall produces healthy grasslands and ensures a food supply of seeds, nuts, and other mast, berries, and other fruits. Although the birds attempt to hatch during dry years, mortality may be as high as 86 percent of juveniles and 70 percent of adults. Winter and summer rainfall is critical to their survival; during periods of extreme drought, the birds may not attempt to nest at all. The lack of rain may account for strange fall dispersal some years. Researchers, for example, report hunters in New Mexico and Texas recovering leg bands from birds that had traveled from 10 to 25 miles each. One moved an astonishing 60 miles.

In southwestern New Mexico, which each year receives only 15 to 20 inches of rain on average, a good place to find scaled quail is near water. State law prohibits hunting any closer than 300 yards from stock watering tanks, so as not to disturb cattle, but the troughs and adjacent windmills are targets to

Stock watering tanks are good places to look for tracks, droppings, and feathers—all signs that scaled quail are in the area.

consider scouting. The birds leave a lot of tracks, and many times friends and I have found them nearby. The average winter home range of scaled quail, in Oklahoma at least, is only about 50 acres.

In Texas and New Mexico where it is legal, hunters sometimes ride around in pickups with unloaded guns out of the case while looking for a covey of blue quail that is feeding, dusting, or going to roost. Scaled quail often fly as a group early in the day when they leave the roost and late in the afternoon when they return. At other times you must train your eyes to spot them on the ground next to pastures, weed-fringed waterways, or around stock watering tanks.

Habitat of the scaled and bobwhite quail overlap in many places. This pair was shot from the Cimarron National Grassland in southwestern Kansas.

As is true with the other love-to-run species of western quail, the key is to bust the covey, then mark the singles and doubles that will likely hold long enough for your dog to point them or for you to move into shooting range. If you can leave the truck and load your gun in time, you might get the typical 10- to 30-bird covey to flush. I have never succeeded in gaining much ground on a running scaled quail, but sometimes shooting in the air will put the little gray streaks aloft. Individuals separated from the covey, especially when roosting time nears, impart a two-note sound that—to my ears, any-way—sounds like *chip-chew, chip-chew.*

A young New Mexico hunter took this scaled quail on grazed BLM land. Note the yucca plant nearby.

THE GAMBEL QUAIL

The Gambel or desert quail typically frequents dusty arroyos and dried-out washes. Creosote bush, mesquite, cholla cactus, and prickly pear comprise the higher vegetation. Apache plume and sacaton grass may grow along the thirsty streambeds. The birds often share home range with scaled quail, al-though individual coveys stay segregated. The inexperienced eye has trouble differentiating such habitat nuances in places like southeastern Arizona and southwestern New Mexico where scaled and Gambel quail both live.

Male Gambel quail have two black, comma-like head feathers that sepa-rate when rubbed between fingers. The hens sport a smaller, single feather. Cockbirds carry the most color: black foreheads, brick-colored caps, upper breasts of gray descending to buff, underwings a chestnut pattern streaked with white.

Hunting tactics are similar to blue quail: run, then gun. I'd rather walk for birds, but there are times when I'd give five bucks just to ride on a tailgate for five minutes. I once heard about the ultimate southwestern quail bird dog, an Arizona Brittany that knew enough to outflank running quail—both Gambel and scaled. The dog ran the old end-around trick, then, facing the hunters, pinned birds into freezing. I've heard that beeper collars and certain whistles

Gambel quail roosters are easily identified by their rufous-colored caps and black feather that looks like a comma.

that sound like screaming hawks will stop running quail cold but have never seen the trick myself. The rallying cry of the Gambel quail is a three-note *chi-ga-go*.

The best Gambel quail hunting is in southern and western Arizona where hunters kill one to two million birds each year when populations are high. Fair to good numbers occur in southeastern California, southern New Mexico, and western Texas. Extreme south-central Utah has a few birds, as does southern Nevada and southwestern Colorado. The Mexican states of Baja California, Sinaloa, and Sonora host hunting seasons, and there are a few desert quail on the islands of Hawaii, Lanai, and Kahoolawe.

Both Gambel and scaled quail live in the desert grasslands of southeastern Arizona.

This New Mexico birdhunter shot a Gambel quail with the help of his Brittany spaniels.

The Gambel is a quail of the southwestern deserts. It is similar in appearance to the valley or California quail.

Successful breeding is also dependent on annual precipitation, with winter rainfall critical. The moisture helps develop green plants such as vetches, filarees, and other ground-covering legumes that quail prefer. Green plant matter translates to vitamin A, which stimulates reproductive organs. Like scaled quail, Gambels are highly opportunistic when it comes to food. A New Mexico study of 57 Gambel crops, for example, found 87 plant species.

THE MEARNS QUAIL

Also called the Montezuma or harlequin quail, the Mearns is a shy, hold-tight bird of the savanna and pinyon pine/live-oak hills of 5,000 feet altitude or higher in the Santa Ritas, Rubies, Mules, Whetstones, Huachucas, and other ranges of southeastern Arizona. I have hunted them a number of times in the San Pedros Mountains region and in the Coronado National Forest near Nogales and Patagonia. In New Mexico they frequent the Capitan, Sacramento, San Mateo, Mogollon, and Black Mountain ranges. They also live throughout much of northern Mexico.

Mearns quail live along mountain slopes in southern New Mexico and southeastern Arizona.

Few upland gamebirds can match the handsome Mearns quail rooster.

Arizona hunters may take 50,000 birds or more in a season, and in New Mexico the harvest may be much higher. Females are an overall buff color, similar to the hue of a hen pheasant, except the breast is a mottled brown with white chin and throat. The roosters are striking with their buckskin-colored crests, white faces, and swirls of black under the eyes and over the cheeks. White polka dots over a brown-black belly give a crouching male the look of a Russian Easter egg. Hunting the Mearns is lung-busting, charley-horse-begging work because the soft, crumbly hills where they live are 45 degrees or more.

Mearns are as similar to Gambel and scaled quail as pecans are to persimmons. The coveys are small, averaging five or six members, and the birds so dispersed and adept at eluding predators that if you can move five coveys in a day you have had a good hunt. Mearns don't care much for seeds; diggers of tubers and roots, they have long toenails and well-developed legs. They run into tall grass and crouch, and without a good dog, you'll rarely find them. They flush by leaping into the air, then exploding into flight. Shooting them as they dodge through openings of live oak is as sporting as it gets.

A feeding covey leaves a lot of sign. Look for disturbed soil, like a tiny rototiller passed through, especially in shaded areas where the soil is a bit moist. Throughout the day Mearns often work their way uphill, scratching, feeding, preening, and resting as they go. In late afternoon they return to roosting areas of wheat-colored grass.

One of the reasons I like to hunt southwestern quail is that I am always learning something. On my last hunt in Arizona, for example, I proved that a dogless hunter can flush Mearns quail if he moves slowly and stops often. I was halfway up a hill when three birds erupted without warning in my face, and I recovered in time to bag one.

Mearns quail are hard to find, even if you locate evidence of their scratching for food.

High-country slopes containing live oak and pinyon pine are prime Mearns quail habitat. Dogless hunters should move and stop slowly.

THE VALLEY QUAIL

Range of the valley or California quail extends from southern Oregon through California to Baja Mexico, but biologists with state game departments have successfully introduced them elsewhere in the West. Valley quail habitat is usually brush-choked ravines and river bottoms in farming areas. Opportunistic feeders, they switch back and forth from grain crops to wild foods but are rarely caught in the open more than a short dash from cover. In winter, large coveys form, numbering 100 or more birds. They roost in heavy brush and are reluctant to leave when threatened.

California, with an annual harvest that sometimes exceeds one million birds, has the best hunting. Washington and Oregon are next, followed by Nevada and Idaho. Good numbers live in British Columbia and Baja Mexico. Limited hunting opportunities occur in Utah, Arizona, and Hawaii. I have hunted valley quail in California along mountain foothills covered with thick, dense chapparal, and in Nevada along farmland irrigation ditches clogged with grease brush, tumbleweeds, and tule grass.

At one time the valley and Gambel quail were one and the same. Speciation occurred a million or more years ago when the Sierra Nevadas uplifted to iso-

The valley quail closely resembles its cousin, the Gambel quail. However, valley quail prefer foothills with brush.

Farming areas with cover are good places to try for valley quail. They roost in heavy brush and are reluctant to leave when threatened.

late birds. Gambels evolved on the desert floor; valley quail flourished in the foothills. The males of both species carry topknots that look like black commas, but—as mentioned—Gambel cocks have black patches on their bellies and rust-colored caps. Valley males sport caps of dark brown, brown throats, and speckled feathering on the nape of their necks. Like her Gambel counterpart, the valley hen sports a tiny paintbrush on her head.

Better hunting occurs on farmland adjacent to heavy cover. Find a covey by listening for their sounds (an *ut, ut* feeding call or *cu-ca-kow* coveying call), searching for tracks and feathers around water or in dust bowls, or asking people familiar with the country. The midmorning to midafternoon hours often provide the best hunting because birds will be out of the roost and feeding or loafing in more-open cover. Even more so than Gambels, flushed valley quail fly low to the ground. Scaled quail, on the other hand, fly much higher.

THE MOUNTAIN QUAIL

At eight to ten ounces each, the mountain species is the largest quail on the continent. Both sexes have a split-feathered plume above their heads, but on the male it is much larger—about three inches. Slate-blue in color, both sexes exhibit bar markings of chestnut and white ahead of the wings and on the lower chest. A single white bar marking to each side of the face frames a throat patch of brick-red on these beautiful birds. You can hunt mountain quail in California, Oregon, Washington, Nevada, and Baja, Mexico. California has the best hunting, but birds are spread out in small populations throughout mountainous habitat in about half the state.

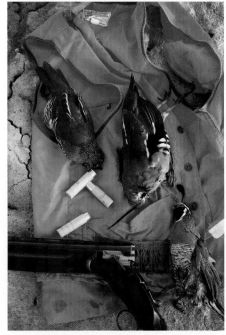

These are tough-to-hunt birds. They favor brush-choked stream bottoms a mile or more above sea level. In Nevada I found them in the Pine Nut Mountains at 7,500 feet, just below snowline, one cold January morning. The birds were feeding along a dried streambed flanked with mountain sage, bunchgrass, and

The mountain quail (center) is much larger than the other quail species. The other birds in the photo are valley quail.

rabbitbrush in an area where pinyon and juniper crawled up the 60-degree slopes. I saw them running ahead of my setter and when they flushed, I marked down a single and a group of three birds. They held for the reflush.

I don't know what those birds were eating because I wanted to get the pair I collected mounted and didn't open their crops. When snow is deep in the canyons, though, mountain quail often move into the sagebrush flats to find food. Although they will eat grain from crop fields, pine nuts, fruits, seeds, grass, forbs, and legumes are more common foods.

As you might suspect by now, keys to success include (1) finding the covey, (2) breaking it up on the flush, and (3) marking the singles for a reflush. If you can't find members of the broken covey, listen for the coveying cry—a three-note *kow-kow-kow.*

THE IMPORTANCE OF CONDITIONING

You'll want to be in good shape to hunt western quail. One hunter I know who sought bobwhite and scaled quail in west Texas wore a pedometer for three days and logged 9.1, 9.0, and 8.9 miles respectively. It is possible to

You have to be in good condition to hunt western quail. These running scaled quail are proof.

walk much farther. You should pack chaps for protection from the mesquite, pricklypear, and occasional clumps of cholla cactus, tasajillo, and holly you will encounter in many places. Lightweight leather boots, thin shooting gloves, and a vest or light jacket provide comfort in temperatures that typically range from 30 to 50 degrees during the late season.

The way I figure it, if you're going to travel west of the Mississippi, you might as well pack the same gun and loads you use for bobwhite hunting. Last January I got lucky: I was able to sandwich hunts for bobwhite and scaled quail in west Texas and Gambel quail in southwestern New Mexico around being the dutiful spouse at a professional conference with my wife in Seattle and my work as a reporter at a trade show in Las Vegas.

Now, months later, events of the conference and show are a blur. The quail hunting experiences, on the other hand, are clear snapshots of joy. I can still see the enormous covey of blue quail that rocketed up and away from the Texas mesquite and flew a hundred yards before dropping into a wide swatch of tabosa grass. A big, rangy chocolate-ticked pointer named Spike nailed them there in the knee-high grass. Spike cast wide, like a spray-gun painter hosing a barn wall, then snapped to—again and again—while we three gunners moved through the scattered singles and took out seven birds.

And it takes little prodding to relive that day shortly thereafter in New Mexico's upper Sonoran Desert when three of us swept through a field of tumbleweeds and old sunflowers gone to seed. Tig (as in "Tiger") and Curly scoured the cover like the vacuum cleaners that Brittanys are, the Gambel quail flushed close underfoot, and the smell of gunpowder wafted on the still air while the sun stopped low in the west for a delicious moment. We had already taken 24 birds that morning, and it was a good thing that someone now said, "Stop! Count your kills." So we did and found we had 20 more quail, one short of a three-man daily limit of 45. Imagine! And this was no hunting preserve. We broke open the guns then and flushed another dozen desert quail on our way back to the truck.

If you hunt birds, you know about such memories. Airports and convention hotels come and go; covey rises linger.

CHAPTER

13

The Ptarmigans

Three races of ptarmigan—the rock, willow, and white-tailed—may be the least gunned gamebirds in the world. Snow grouse, as ptarmigan are often called, are circumpolar in their distribution. Native range in Scandinavia, Mongolia, Siberia, and North America is, roughly, between the 52nd and 83rd parallels of latitude. Winter migrants are found as far south as Newfoundland and northern Ontario and there are small but stable populations in a few states along the spine of the Rockies. The three races have many subspecies.

The willow ptarmigan inhabits river valleys where willow, larch, and stunted spruce and aspen grow. Look for them in evergreen copses, sedge meadow wetlands, and brushy saddles between hills—all near tundra willow turning orange with September frost and within a mile or so of a major waterway. I have hunted willow ptarmigan several times in the Far North of Quebec and in Alaska. They are also plentiful in the Yukon and Northwest Territories and northern British Columbia.

The rock ptarmigan prefers an even bleaker landscape of lichen-covered rocks, boulders, and outcroppings, but habitats tend to overlap with the wil-

The male willow ptarmigan in its summer coat is a piebald bird of white underparts and chestnut-colored back, neck, and head. It is similar in appearance to the red grouse of Scotland, which does not turn all-white in winter.

low ptarmigan. I have photographed rock ptarmigan in the Northwest Territories above the Arctic Circle, but I have never shot one.

The white-tailed ptarmigan is smaller than the bigger rock and willow species, which are about the size of small ruffed grouse. The white-tailed is an alpine bird that lives in the Rockies and other western mountain ranges and is similar in size to a pigeon. The only white-tailed ptarmigan I ever shot was a Colorado bird I killed at just under 13,000 feet during a cross-country odyssey to take a North American grouse grand slam. Colorado, Utah, and California have huntable populations. Releases of willow ptarmigan in Montana and a couple of other western states either failed or did not produce enough birds to warrant hunting.

The white-tailed ptarmigan, shown here in summer plumage, is an alpine bird about the size of a barn pigeon.

Alaska offers the best opportunity to bag all three species; in fact, a friend of mine, who happens to be a wildlife biologist, did it in a single day and within a mile of a major highway. The last time I looked, the bag limits were generous (20 birds daily) and the season long (mid-August to mid-April).

THE OVERLOOKED GAMEBIRD

Most upland hunters never consider ptarmigan because of the birds' often harsh and inaccessible environment. Subsistence hunters kill most of the 300,000 or so that biologists estimate are harvested each year in North America. However, the red grouse, which is one of 16 subspecies of the willow ptarmigan and which does not turn all-white in winter, is revered in Europe. The Norwegian National Field Trials are held on willow ptarmigan each year. The Glorious Twelfth (August 12) is one of Great Britain's most celebrated events, when shooters in Scotland open the season on driven birds. It is expensive sport.

In a time when populations of quail, woodcock, pheasants, ruffed grouse, and plains grouse rise or fall with the fickleness of nature and the govern-

The Colorado Rockies is one of the few places in the continental United States to hunt the white-tailed ptarmigan.

ment's farm programs, ptarmigan offer steady sport. They are the perfect gamebird for training a young dog, offer a sporting challenge, and are very good to eat. Whenever I plan to hunt caribou or fish for Arctic char, I pack my dog, shotgun, and at least two boxes of shells, and I am happy to report that a growing number of outfitters now offer ptarmigan hunting.

On a long hunting expedition to Alaska many years ago, I ran into flocks of willow ptarmigan while hunting moose along the Post River drainage in the Kuskokwim Mountains. Later, ptarmigan woke us every morning with their feeding calls of *go-back, go-back* on the Alaska Peninsula where we stalked caribou and fished for silver salmon. We shot a few ptarmigan, but it wasn't too sporting because the birds had no fear of us. Then I began to hunt them with a pointing dog.

My Brittany found the only white-tailed ptarmigan I saw in Colorado during that high country hunt when a partner of mine suffered altitude sickness and had to descend. The real test came a few years later in Quebec's Ungava region. Three of us planned a caribou hunting trip to a new area that had just opened on the Diana River about 30 miles northwest of Kuujjuaq. Old Fort Chimo, as it is often called, is a little blip on the tundra where 1,200 people live about 900 miles straight north of Montreal.

"In late August when you come," said Joe Stefanski, who runs the camp and owns High Arctic Adventures, "the fishing for brook trout and arctic char should be superb. With luck the Leaf River herd of caribou will be moving through, and you'll see muskox although they're protected."

"Any ptarmigan?" I wondered.

"Oh, yeah. They're everywhere. Bring a dog and a shotgun if you want to."

So I packed a young English setter, a 28-gauge, and a couple boxes of shells. My two partners brought a .410 and a 20-gauge. When they ran out of shells, we took turns with my gun until we used up all the 28-gauge ammo, too. We had all the action we could handle. The camp's Inuit guide, Isaac Angnatuk, had never seen a dog hunt birds. Isaac was amazed at how Sherlock, my young setter, handled his first-ever points and retrieves. The 300 birds we saw that first day were heady stuff for a young recruit and the perfect opportunity to staunch my dog, mold his tail straight up, and work on releasing and retrieving. He went from kindergarten to fourth grade by noon; at day's end he was well into high school.

That night three Frenchmen camping up the river joined us for dinner at the lodge. "We shot seven ptarmigan today with our 12-gauge," they said.

Much of the world is tundra and therefore home to ptarmigan. This scene is in Quebec's remote Far North.

"Took 'em right on the ground when they walked through camp. You don't need a dog to kill ptarmigan." Isaac looked at me and grinned. Like me, he was probably thinking, *If they only knew the fun they were missing.*

Devoto was right: There is no such thing as uninteresting landscape. Snow grouse appear to live in a land of nothing—extreme emptiness, glacier-strewn rocks, dwarf larch, the broad sweep of tundra, the wind constantly coming at you in a place where weather is made, a world of extremes. Then, suddenly, the brooding sky is full of life—a ptarmigan flock, white wings and queer cackling sounds everywhere it seems. This is elemental sport in an elemental place that looks exactly as it did when some ancestor leaned on a spear and squinted to watch herds on the horizon. I love this nothing-and-everything land of ptarmigan. It is land too beautiful to be devoid of a gamebird.

A SPECIALIZED BIRD

Ptarmigan are gregarious birds that stay in family units until the tundra starts to turn orange with frost. Then, the families join to build flocks that can number several hundred birds by winter. Strong flyers, ptarmigan may migrate 300

Sherlock returns with a willow ptarmigan. Note the habitat of food and escape cover right near the water.

miles or more to find food. In early fall they gorge themselves on blueberries and crowberries. Like deer, they browse on the most tender and most succulent thumbnail-sized leaves of dwarf willow, of which there are some 25 species that grow along the flood plains of far north rivers. Although ptarmigan will migrate well below treeline, they are most often associated with tundra. Given their circumpolar range and the fact that six percent of the planet is tundra, ptarmigan have a lot of places to live.

Tom Huggler holds a willow ptarmigan.

Wonderfully equipped with feathered feet (*Lagopus,* the family name, is from the Greek, meaning "hare-footed" or covered) and strong wings, the ptarmigan has plumage with higher insulating qualities than most other birds because when fluffed, the feathers are designed to trap more air. Tiny hairlike feathers in their nostrils help to warm frigid air before inhaling. Even though these adaptations enable ptarmigan to withstand their harsh environment, the bird's world is fragile and life is tenuous at best. Aerial and ground predators plunder egg, chick, and adult. An estimated 60 to 80 percent of first nesting attempts fail, and the growing season is so short that ptarmigan dare waste no time if renesting is to be successful. Willow ptarmigan are the only monogamous grouse, and the males are perfectly capable of raising hatched chicks to maturity.

A SPECIAL QUARRY

The sport can be fairly easy, even luxurious. Perhaps only bobwhite quail are as accommodating to the sleep-in gunner. Like those wonderful little birds, ptarmigan run and hold for the dog. But these birds are like prairie grouse, too, because they use their eyes to spot danger and have powerful wings for escape, often flying a half-mile or more. Their flap-and-glide pattern of flight is similar to sharptails and prairie chickens, as is that queer *kuk-kuk-kuk* sound that floats out over open ground.

And ptarmigan are not always easy. I have tramped for miles across the tundra and flushed nothing but snow buntings. I have glassed river valleys in

Ptarmigan are accommodating gamebirds for training young dogs.

search of moose and caribou and never spotted a ptarmigan. Like other upland gamebirds, ptarmigan occupy niches within the greater habitat. You have to find them and when you do, escape cover will probably be close by.

Recently I returned with Sherlock (and three boxes of shells this time) to Joe Stefanski's camp. On its rush north to Ungava Bay, the Diana River opens wide to create five-mile-long Diana Lake. One day with guide Kevin Kane at the helm, we motored south, upriver, for 45 minutes in the camp boat, an 18-foot Lund pushed by a 30-horse Yamaha. The lake necks down into a river again where it flashes around bus-sized boulders and hides trout in deep holes. Kevin took us to the upstream limit where the river plunges down a 15-foot-high waterfall and creates a deafening roar. Below the cascade, short-stopped brookies to three pounds each gang up. They will exhaust you if you let them.

My two friends and I didn't. After a couple hours of fishing, we talked Kevin into dropping us off about three miles from camp. With Sherlock leading the charge, we bird hunters fanned out across the tundra and hunted our way home. We were not alone. Wolf scat suggested another predator had been here. Above us in a storm-clouded sky, a peregrine falcon hovered on tippling wings, waiting for us to flush its favorite meal. The peregrine reminded me of one of those red-tailed hawks that shadow hunters on a game preserve.

We shot 20 ptarmigan, including one "suddenly salad" bird that Siegfried Gagnon, my friend from Montreal, erased at close range with his Spanish-made .410 double gun. I've always considered the .410 to be an under-achiever, but in the capable hands of Siegfried, there is no debate. I witnessed him kill birds cleanly at 40 yards with that little popgun. I was toting my 28-gauge Winchester over-and-under, and shooting No. 7 one-half shot in a one-ounce load. Gerry Bethge, a magazine editor and friend, carried a 12-gauge Citori.

The birds were plentiful, and we filled our game bags. After awhile, I sought only the bigger, adult birds because they flew harder and were more challenging. Later, I hunted only with my camera. One day Sherlock pointed a ptarmigan 20 inches from his nose. He held the point for 10 minutes while we snapped pictures. When I moved in for the flush, Sher-lock—unable to restrain himself any longer—pounced. Holding the bird in his mouth, he took a couple of steps and went on point again. Gerry was squatting, trying to get the perfect photograph; suddenly the bird being pointed flushed. When Sherlock opened his mouth, that bird flew. Gerry dropped his camera, shot twice and missed twice. I wish I had brought

Gerry Bethge (foreground) and Siegfried Gagnon move in on a point.

along a videocam for that unbelievable incident—the bird that brought Gerry to his knees.

Toward the end of our week, Sherlock and I accompanied three dogless hunters from Massachusetts who had come here solely to hunt ptarmigan. I took pictures and worked on my setter's ranging and retrieving. Our best day was 32 birds in the bag. It is for experiences like these that I love to hunt ptarmigan.

PLANNING TIPS

All-rubber Wellingtons are perfect boots for ptarmigan hunting in the muskeg tundra. If you wear traditional footwear, bring a spare pair, along with boot dryers. You'll need gloves, a warm hat, raingear, and insulated underwear because the average daily temperature in July is only about 50 degrees up around the 58th parallel. However, be prepared for warm days, too. You will be hunting in late August or September. At times, I have needed insect repellent for blackflies and mosquitoes. The next day it may snow four inches.

Seasons typically open in August when young birds may be barely fledged. September is a better time to go, but the weather then is less predictable. Another option may be spring hunting, when the males sport bright red eye combs.

If you book with an outfitter, be sure to ask for updated conditions, and don't settle for the general forecast that insists, "No problem. There are always ptarmigan around." Local population crashes can and do occur and are based on weather conditions, predator populations, and food scarcity. You should also ask the outfitter if he intends to keep tabs on ptarmigan numbers and if he is willing to fly you into areas where birds are more plentiful should they be hard to find near your camp.

Knock on wood, I suppose, but I've never had to deal with a lost firearm or—worse yet—a lost dog when traveling by air to Canada. In fact, baggage handlers and ticket takers alike have gone out of their way to make sure my dog has been treated well.

No one can control the weather, and air travelers have fewer recourses than ever it seems when flights get delayed for any number of reasons. Still, we sportsmen can minimize problems. First, before leaving home have all your paperwork in order: (1) passport or birth certificate, (2) U.S. Customs registration of your firearm(s), (3) current health certificate and proof of rabies vaccination for your dog. Second, use clear carton tape or one of those see-through bill of lading pouches to attach information about the dog to the air freight kennel. Include the dog's name and a couple of photos and list emergency contact information, including the name, address, and phone number of your vet. Third, split your ammunition between luggage containers (it is illegal to pack ammo with a firearm); in the event one is lost, you'll still be able to shoot. Finally, pack any medicine, documents, basic toiletries, and a change of clothing into a carry-on bag.

CHAPTER 14

The Doves and Pigeons

Mourning doves are the most plentiful gamebird in North America. According to research by the U.S. Fish & Wildlife Service, which is charged with managing migratory gamebirds, the continental population in autumn ranges from 400 to 475 million. The annual national harvest of some 50 million doves in the 39 states with hunting seasons is larger than any other gamebird. This seemingly huge bag of about 10 percent, incidentally, has virtually no impact on the overall population because 65 to 70 percent of the birds die of natural causes before they see their first birthday anyway.

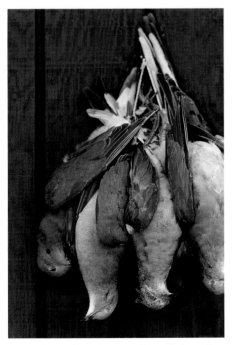

The 50 million mourning doves that American hunters harvest nationally each year have little impact on the huge continental population of more than 400 million birds.

This high mortality rate is why Nature has arranged for doves to mate often and regularly. A pair of doves may rear several broods of offspring during the long breeding season, which begins as early as March and lasts until late summer. Hunting seasons typically begin on September 1, and some states enjoy late season hunting opportunities as well. The daily bag is usually 10 to 15 doves per hunter.

Unfortunately, I can't hunt mourning doves in my native Michigan, where they have been protected as songbirds since 1905. If you'll allow a brief digression, it amazes me how misinformation can span a whole century. The passenger pigeon, a cousin to the dove, became extinct in Michigan and other northern forested states a century ago for two reasons: (1) lumbermen destroyed the birds' habitats of mature timber, and (2) commercial market hunters overshot them in the days before hunting regulations. The mourning dove is a different species with different habitat needs than the passenger pigeon. Doves are more plentiful today than ever before because rural farming habitats are more to their liking. Current high populations have nothing to do with the long hunting ban.

I like to hunt birds because of the exercise involved, the sporting aspects of flushing and shooting at winged game, the joy of being with my dogs and my family and friends, the opportunity to experience and understand the natural world. The dove rates high for all of these reasons. Many wing shooters rate the hard-to-hit dove the number one challenge. I have hunted mourning doves in Indiana since 1984 when the season first opened there. I have shot doves in North Dakota and South Dakota, too, but never in the South where droves of dove hunters eagerly anticipate the opening day of hunting season, just as their fathers and grandfathers did.

SIMPLE, INEXPENSIVE SPORT

Dove shooting appeals strongly to thousands of upland hunters because it is the first season of the new hunting year even though autumn is weeks away.

Dove hunters need little equipment to participate in this simple, fun sport.

Early September is not too late to work on your wing shooting prowress. If your retriever or pointer needs a tune-up on obedience or finding and retrieving downed birds, bring the dog along. Dove shooting is ideal sport for women, young hunters, and novice shooters of all ages. Disabled sportmen and women find the dove to be the most accommodating of all upland gamebirds, and it is inexpensive as well.

You don't need special equipment or clothing—a little camo, a gun, and a box of shells. Maybe two boxes because the smallish, hard-flying dove is a real challenge to take on the wing. If my memory is correct, I shot only nine birds while firing a box of 25 shells on that first-ever dove hunt in Indiana. Some hunters perform better; many do worse.

HOW TO HIT DOVES

At only five or six ounces, the mourning dove is a small target that averages 10 or 11 inches long, half of which is a pointed tail. Fragile birds, doves need little punch to bring down. Target loads of No. 7½, 8, or even 9 shot in the smaller gauges are fine, but there is nothing wrong with shooting a 12-gauge or even a blackpowder shotgun for that matter. I personally prefer lighter guns with 28- or 29-inch barrels because I find they are better balanced and allow me to swing through more easily. Improved cylinder or modified is the

Veteran wing shooters rate the acrobatic dove among the trickiest targets to hit.

choke of choice, unless you want to try your hand at 40-yard streaks of gray, for which you will need a full choke pattern.

The key to hitting these dipping, diving targets is to learn to shoot instinctively. If you can get on a sustained flight line of birds coming in to eat, drink, or roost, you can literally point your left foot (assuming you are right-handed) at the spot where you hope to kill the bird. That foot becomes the anchor point for your stance, which involves leaning forward a bit from the knees up and preparing to pivot your body to take the shot when it is offered. The next step is keep the gun in the ready position—looking over the barrel(s) while making sure the index finger is along the trigger guard, the thumb is on the safety, and the butt plate is jammed against your ribs. Mount the gun to shoulder in one fluid motion, without moving your head, and make sure you lock the top of your thumb under the cheekbone.

Then, as though pointing at the bird with your left hand on the forearm of your gun, paint through the target and squeeze off a shot. Don't worry about lead—it is built into the instinctive method. In fact, if you think about leading doves you will miss them. You will also burn hulls and not touch feathers if you track incoming birds and try to trace their erratic flight patterns. Simply mount, swing, and shoot in one fluid motion, and you'll likely improve your score.

HUNTING TACTICS

Warm, Indian summer afternoons are the perfect time to post a field of sunflowers, chisel-plowed corn, disked weeds or harvested wheat, soybeans or milo—all preferred dove foods. Morning hours are good times, too, but I like the afternoons better, when the day's heat is going, not coming. It doesn't take much detective work to find where doves are feeding. Look for them entering and leaving fields, resting on nearby power lines, and parked in trees overlooking cut fields of grain. Binoculars help pinpoint their movements and aid in telling doves apart from other birds. When water is scarce, watch for them to concentrate around ponds and livestock tanks. Keep an eye open for stands of pine and other conifers, which they often choose as roosting sites.

Although you can walk up feeding doves with or without your dog, this is a bird built for the pass shooter. The key is to size up a field the doves are using and make sure you take a stand well before your scouting tells you they will likely appear. Choose a stand that affords as much visibility as possible because doves sometimes pour in from all compass points. A lone tree, preferably dead, in the middle of the field is often the best spot. Doves like to perch there for awhile and look over the banquet table before flying down to feed.

Taking a stand in the middle of a crop field affords full visibility and helps in spotting incoming doves. Be sure to set up well before you expect birds to arrive.

A solitary tree in the middle of a feeding zone is the perfect place to take a stand for doves.

Other covers worth considering within a field are a small patch of woods, a wet spot with cattails or other vegetation, rock island with head-high sumac, slough with ragweed, or brushy draw. Perimeter cover of woods, weeds, or brush will help hide you, too, except you won't see those come-from-behind birds unless a partner, who is in a position to know, warns you. A farmer in North Dakota one day showed me the best spot to post on his sprawling wheatfield. "That dead cottonwood, right there," he motioned from the cab of his idling tractor to an enormous snag along the field edge. "They always head for that old tree." And he was right: I shot a limit that afternoon and hardly moved my feet.

Binoculars aid in identifying the smallish dove.

PUBLIC HUNTING AREAS

Private farmlands offer good dove shooting in many areas, but getting to hunt on them can be hard because crops are usually still standing in the early season. Also, some landowners do not consider the dove a gamebird. For these reasons, consider checking out your state's public hunting areas.

Wildlife biologists in Indiana, for example, plant sunflowers in food plots from one-half acre to 10 acres each on 17 properties specifically managed for doves and other wildlife. Workers mow strips to each side of the sunflower rows, which may be 500 feet long and 12 to 30 rows wide. The sunflowers attract hordes of doves, and the strips aid in locating downed birds.

It is probably legal to hunt doves in crop fields, but check your state's regulations to be sure. Larry Cook, a friend of mine from Indiana, manages about 10 acres of his father's 80-acre farm each year for doves. In late August Larry disks down wheat stubble or a fallow field of weeds to attract hungry birds. In a typical year he and his friends shoot 400 doves there.

State wildlife personnel often manage public hunting areas for doves.

AN INDIANA HUNT FOR DOVES

In northern states, the best hunting occurs during the first few days of the season before the doves migrate. In mid-September last year, for example, a Hoosier friend and I enjoyed some fast shooting for an hour for doves that poured into a harvested cornfield, but I didn't think it was going to turn out that way. The day before I had seen dozens, shoulder to shoulder, on power lines near my home about a hundred miles north and east. There were a few at my birdfeeder, too, when I last filled it. Fresh travelers no doubt replace early migrants, and some doves, of course, stay all winter if they have a reliable source of food.

On this warm Sunday afternoon, my shorthair and I watched the wind stir the bromegrass under the center-pivot irrigation rig where we waited for targets. It was a good setup: the landowner had recently cut the 100-acre field of seed corn, leaving plenty of food on the ground. To the east were several stands of mature pines, ideal dove roosts. To the south lay a pair of gravel pits, assuring grit and water.

While waiting, I noticed a ladybug moving along the black tread of a huge tire next to me. Suddenly, the little spot of orange turned to cross the

T on "Titan." Where was the ladybug going in such a hurry, I wondered. And why?

Gunfire distracted me. Hidden behind the next tire about 20 yards away, my host, Jon Howard, dropped a pair of doves with two shots. A couple of paper mache decoys that Jon had hung from overhead pipes on the irrigation rig apparently had worked.

When I turned back to the tire, the ladybug was gone, replaced by an excited, dime-sized spider that reminded me of the one dog back home in his kennel. I wondered if spiders could smell and if the ladybug would get away. After all, the harvest season was at hand.

Jon's yelp brought me to attention in time to take a snapshot at a dove streaking by my stand. Amazingly, I killed the bird on a long shot with my 28-gauge over-and-under.

Dove shooting is among the earliest of the upland gamebird seasons. It's the ideal sport for sharpening your shooting eye and giving your dog a training exercise.

This dribble of doves turned into a sustained dinner flight as birds suddenly appeared in pairs and small bunches. By the time the shadow of the tire completely engulfed me, we had collected 23 birds, seven short of a two-man limit. I marinated them in a mixture of garlic powder and Worchestershire sauce with just enough olive oil to carry the mixture. Then I grilled them medium-rare. I recommend a good cabernet sauvignon.

THE WHITE-WINGED DOVE

White-winged doves are larger and heavier than mourning doves, have a white-tipped, squared tail, and white wing patches, which show up in flight. A true bird of the arid Southwest, where they subsist mostly on the seeds of desert plants, whitewings may travel long distances for water. Good places to lie in wait for them are near livestock ponds and watering tanks where the birds gather early and late in the day. Hunters seek them along with mourning doves in southeastern California, southern Arizona, southwestern New Mexico, and southern Texas. Better shooting occurs in Mexico, where most of the whitewings go in winter. California uplanders may also shoot spotted doves and ringed turtledoves.

A brace of white-winged doves. White-wings inhabit the arid Southwest, and subsist on the seeds of desert plants.

The band-tailed pigeon is a little-known upland gamebird that provides great sport for pass-shooters.

THE BAND-TAILED PIGEON

The band-tailed pigeon lives in coastal forests of hardwoods and conifers from southern British Columbia through California to Baja Mexico. They are also found in mountain forests of the Rockies and other ranges in Utah, Colorado, Arizona, and New Mexico. Hunters may legally seek them in Utah, Oregon, and California, but they kill very few. The annual harvest in Utah, for example, is usually 100 birds or less. Also called the wild pigeon, blue pigeon, and white-collared pigeon, bandtails are about the size of a barn pigeon. Average weight is 12 ounces; length varies from 12 to 16 inches. Males sport a half-ring of white on the back of their necks. Otherwise, the sexes look alike: purple-gray on the head, neck, and breast fading to white toward the belly, an upper back of green-gray, a lower back of blue-gray. The tail is a dark gray with a lighter-colored gray band. Feet and bill are yellow, except the tip of the bill is black.

Females typically nest in conifers, building a platform of twigs within 20 feet of the ground, and lay only one egg. Preferred foods include seeds, pine buds, berries, acorns, evergreen needles, and insects. The best way to hunt bandtails is to find a food source or roosting area and ambush them there during the early fall hunting season. If you spot a flight line of migrants, you can also pass-shoot them as they fly over. Friends and I experienced this one time in California during a valley quail hunt.

CHAPTER
15

The Hunting Preserve

Recently returning from two weeks on the road, hunting my way home from Oklahoma, I thought about how lucky I am to hunt gamebirds in so many places and be able to make a living at it. But how long will it last? Will anyone be able to duplicate my experiences in the future?

Call it "road ramblings," if you will, but I worry about such things. In Oklahoma, friends and I flushed 13 coveys of bobwhites one day—on leased land not easily accessible. In Kansas, the only reason we found pheasants and quail on private property where we had permission to hunt was due to the abundance of CRP land. But in Iowa, where fertile farmland fetches more than $150 a rental acre and where half or more of former CRP holdings have been plowed down because of changes in the Farm Bill, my dogs and I did not fare so well.

Government set-aside programs date all the way back to the Soil Bank days of the 1960s. They're the main reason farmland birds like pheasants and quail have managed to hold on in the new corporate world of agribusiness that is not kind to them. Hunting clubs and business-minded sportsmen are leasing private lands at an alarming rate. This practice removes private land from the potential pool and serves to increase hunting pressure on public land.

So I see a future of reduced opportunities for bird hunters, in spite of efforts by Pheasants Forever, Quail Unlimited, the Ruffed Grouse Society, and other conservation groups.

Enter the gamebird hunting preserve.

The national directory called *Black's 2001 Wing & Clay* lists nearly 1,400 such preserves open to the public. They are increasing in number. According to Jim Janson, permit specialist with the Michigan DNR wildlife division, there are 183 gamebird hunting preserves in Michigan, 102 of which are commercial operations open to the public. "We're getting more all the time," Janson says.

"Preserves are helping to keep hunting alive in this country," says John Mullin, 82, who started Arrowhead Shooting Preserve at Goose Lake, Iowa, in 1952. "Some of the more successful operations are those that cater to families and young shooters and involve the community in fun activities like hunter-safety workshops and game dinners."

There are now about 40 gamebird hunting preserves in Iowa. Even South Dakota, a state that once bragged it would never have to grow pheasants and liberate them, now has, according to Mullin, more than 130 commercial preserve operations.

Shooting and hunting preserves offer extended and new opportunities to many upland hunters. This photo was taken at Burnt Pine Plantation in Georgia.

IS PRESERVE HUNTING UNETHICAL?

Last winter I read with amusement an article in the *Detroit Free Press* knocking hunting preserves. The writer, a friend of mine, took to task a Maryland preserve for allowing game hoggery (twenty Washington, D.C. big shots killed 182 ducks) and making a mockery of the sport. My friend wrote, "The best thing we could do with shooting preserves is close them" because they're "the outdoors equivalent of a brothel."

I remember walking out of a wild duck hunting camp in Alaska a few years ago because two members purposely overshot their limits. Some people simply bring their shabby behavior to outdoor sport wherever it is practiced. Preserve hunting doesn't encourage poor sportsmanship any more than catching bluegills from a stocked pond does. In fact, hiring a guide or going to a place where fish and game are released improves your chances at bringing something home. You pay for what you take. If sirloin steaks are on sale at the supermarket and you have the cash and there is no limit, you might decide to stock your freezer.

There is nothing wrong with that.

Preserves provide a safe and fun environment for introducing youngsters to shooting and upland bird hunting.

They afford senior citizens the opportunity to work their dogs and continue hunting. Most preserves are open for six months or more each year.

If my math is right, those Washington hunters shot an average of nine ducks each. Federal regulations generally allow mourning dove hunters to take 15 birds daily in states that have open seasons. That isn't game hoggery either.

We need hunting preserves more than ever before. You can take a kid fishing or hunting only so many times without getting anything before the youngster loses interest altogether. Because preserves provide these and other opportunities, more hunters are going to them, and they are increasing in number.

I hope private land ownership in this country never reaches the point it has in Europe where nearly all hunting is done on managed shooting estates.

In Michigan, at least, that may not happen because nearly one-fourth of our land base—or some 9 million acres—is public or company timberlands enrolled in the Commercial Forest Act and largely open to hunting by law. Half of the real estate in the Upper Peninsula alone is public land. Laws, however, can be changed. If we ever reach the point where hunting on public land is diminished—either through anti-hunting legislation or the loss of game populations—private hunting preserves will figure more strongly than ever.

Two reasons more hunters don't consider preserves now are: (1) the fear of high cost, and (2) the belief that gamebirds and animals are too tame to provide sport. Are these allegations true?

IS PRESERVE HUNTING EXPENSIVE?

Although it's true that some preserve operators charge annual membership fees of $1,000 or more (mostly to corporations), the average cost to join is more like $250. Some owners charge considerably less or offer day memberships, and some don't charge at all. If you are considering paying a membership fee, weigh the benefits offered with those of the competition.

Last spring I hunted one of the many mid-Michigan farms leased by Farmland Pheasant Hunters, Inc., which releases pheasants and quail on the properties it manages. The membership fee is $85 per year, but I had to pay only $25 because I was the guest of a dues-paying member. If I wanted to carry a camera instead of a gun, the fee would have been only $10. Where's the high cost?

And what about the price of birds? We hunted bobwhites only and agreed to a 5-quail limit at $65 per person (a 10-quail limit was $90 each). So for $90 I got to hunt all day, and my young setter practiced his points and I taught him to honor the points of two other young dogs belonging to my friends. Pheasant prices are affordable, too: $57 per person for two birds and $84 for four. Those are weekday rates; weekend rates are $5 less expensive. There are even limited opportunities for deer hunting on some of the farms.

"I wanted to make preserve hunting affordable for as many sportsmen as possible," says Preston Mann, Jr., who started Farmland Pheasant Hunters, Inc. a few years ago. "And I wanted to duplicate the wild experience as much as I could."

Mann gives his hunters, who park in a prescribed area on the landowner's property, a map showing the boundaries. Birds, released the evening before, could be anywhere on the farm. You and your dog have to find them. The only people you're likely to see are members of your own hunting party. No one else may walk the land on the day of your hunt.

IS THE GAME TAME?

Perhaps hunting a deer or boar that has been fed pellets and shelled corn for months, then turned out into a small enclosure for you to stalk, may leave some sport to be desired. I can't say because I have never hunted big game on a preserve. But I have hunted birds—lots of birds, including pheasants, chukar and Hungarian partridge, bobwhite, scaled, and Gambel quail, and even guinea fowl.

Yes, I'd rather hunt wild birds, but most reared birds act wild enough to suit me and my dogs. Those that don't are either released at too young an age or are raised in small, open pens where they learn to herd and have no opportunity to practice flying and other survival skills. I don't like to shoot ringnecks with missing tails, usually the result of confinement or poor handling. Once in awhile you'll experience birds too fat to fly well. These conditions, plus a cold rain, tend to keep birds on the ground instead of in the air where you want them.

On the other hand, one of the best times to hunt pheasants is in March and April when the roosters are so unpredictable they may run right off the property. Like in any other business there are preserve operators who do their job well, and some who run a sloppy system. My advice is to get references and check them out before booking a hunt.

Many hunting preserve owners are members of the North American Gamebird Association, which constantly seeks to improve the quality of stock through breeding selection and rearing practices. A few years ago in Dallas I spoke at the annual NAGA conference and was impressed with the professionalism of its members. These are people determined to enhance preserve hunting to the highest level possible. You might want to check to see if the preserve you're planning to visit is a NAGA member.

There are many other benefits, besides sport hunting, when you join a preserve.

DOG TRAINING

Wild bird hunting seasons usually run for three or four months. Preserves are generally open for business at least eight months of every year (normally from

September through April—check your state's regulations). That translates to plenty of training opportunities for your dog.

All young dogs in training need contact with birds. In the past, I've bought, raised, and released my own stock under DNR permit, but the practice is time-consuming, and I'm not always around to care for the birds. It's easier to take my young charges to a preserve and work them on birds there. Some preserves allow walk-up hunting after driven shoots. Others allow members to work their dogs during off hours for birds unclaimed by previous hunting parties.

Many operators have dog training professionals on-site. For years I had my dogs finish-trained by Dale Jarvis at Hunter's Creek Club in Metamora, one of Michigan's oldest and best-respected preserves, even though I am not a member. If kenneling services are available, they will usually cost less than the boarding fees charged by most veterinary hospitals.

You don't have to own a dog, of course, to hunt on most preserves. Bigger operations have club dogs that go along, with a handler, as part of the hunt. I once bought a hard-hunted Brittany from a preserve—some people whose opinions I respect say he was the best dog I'll ever own.

Bird dogs need to train on live birds. Most preserves have a dog trainer on staff who can work with your dog.

FAMILY PARTICIPATION

Membership has its privileges. Many preserves cater to families, hosting appreciation dinners and bringing in professional speakers to give seminars on how to cook wild game, take better outdoor pictures, and make your dog more obedient. A few have family campgrounds. Some preserves become community service centers for these and other activities, including hunter safety certification courses.

I believe the best place to introduce a youngster, wife, or girlfriend to hunting is at a preserve. They are safe places to learn shooting skills and then practice them. Because birds tend to hold better for the dogs and flush more closely, smaller shotguns like the 20- and 28-gauge are effective. It's far easier to break in a new recruit with a gun that doesn't have the weight or the recoil of a 12-gauge.

Shooting instruction and birds to hunt are just two reasons why young hunters approve of shooting preserves.

SHOOTING INSTRUCTION

Many years ago I participated in a European hunt at a preserve not far from my home. We started the day with a couple rounds of skeet, and then had the chance to hit high-flying pheasants released unannounced while we dozen gunners rotated clockwise to man blinds situated in a big circle. It was a lot of fun, and, once I got the hang of it, I shot quite well.

According to the publishers of *Black's Wing & Clay* directory, more than half of the nation's hunting preserves now offer clay pigeons for shooting instruction. Sporting clay shooting is growing so popular that some preserves actually have two courses and have instructors on hand to give shooting tips. Sporting clays duplicate field hunting conditions, giving shooters practice in learning how to hit surprising shots at tough angles. The sport is teaching a whole new generation of hunters how to be safe and effective shooters.

These, then, are some of the reasons why preserves are figuring more prominently than ever before. Not only is preserve hunting affordable, many sportsmen believe, as I do, that we can't afford not to have them.

WHERE TO GO

Some preserve owners advertise in the Yellow Pages under "Hunting and Fishing Preserves." For a complete list of private and commercial preserves contact your state's wildlife department, which is the agency most likely charged with licensing and regulation.

You can also pick up a current copy of *Black's Wing & Clay*. Published annually by Black's Sporting Directories, the book is a national guide to shotgun shooting instruction, equipment, and hunting and shooting destinations. Your library may have a copy or contact the publisher at P.O. Box 2029, Red Bank, NJ 07701 (phone: 732–224–8700; e-mail: *blacksporting@msn.com*).

EPILOGUE

South Dakota in September on the second hot day of a grasslands hunt for prairie chickens and sharp-tailed grouse: My creaking knees need a shot of WD-40; my tailbone aches from hoofing it up too many hills higher than I thought I could handle. The 28-gauge double, normally light as a toy, feels like a two-by-four on my shoulder. The sun bears down like an angry yellow eye, and the relentless prairie wind sends tear streaks past my ears. Heat flickering over the horizon an eternity away reminds me of my pinched throat and hands so dry the skin flakes away like some molting snake.

Hunting is the last thought on my mind. I'm balancing next month's budget. I am swimming in the motel pool back in Pierre.

Somewhere in that sweep of grass and vault of sky a meadowlark's song floats down on the wind. I pause, trying to locate the bird. I look out past the stirring grass, combed by the wind. Beyond the loping setter, tacking into the breeze. Farther yet to the lion-colored hills, soft and filling now with afternoon shadow. Far away to one side, my two hunting partners are flyspecks crawling over a huge piece of sandpaper. The wind is moaning in the tubes of my shotgun.

A bird has sung liquid, bubbling notes from somewhere in this sea of rusted bluestem. But where? After a long moment I move on, slowly realizing that something has changed. The punishing step-by-step is now an easy cadence, measured and purposeful. The grasshoppers that carom off my nylon pant facings in panicked bursts of yellow are no less significant than the distant puffball clouds with their dark bottoms as heavy as cold-rolled steel.

I belong. The pain in my legs is suddenly gone, not unlike the endorphin fix the marathoner craves. I could walk to the horizon. I nearly do.

A special moment in the uplands: when hunter, dog, and bird all come together.

Every bird hunt has its moment. The moment I savor most is knowing I am inextricably caught up in the hunt. A poet whose name escapes me once described this feeling as the dancer becoming the dance. The sense of great power that comes with such deep connection is countered with a certain loss of power, or control, which is our inability to do anything about it. What we are after, of course, is that final hair's balance on the scale, that last drop in the cup that sends the meniscus over the edge. When the supreme moment occurs, our realization of it is usually subtle but sometimes riveting.

I believe this phenomenon happens to every bird hunter. I know it happens to me.

Such poignant moments get filed away long afterward with the perfect points, the five-for-five mornings, the full-limit days. They occur at any time and in any place, but the fact that the revelations happen often to me whenever I hunt prairie grouse says something about these shy birds that fly on crooked wings. And it speaks even more about the places where they live, grassland vistas where a man is infinitesimal but can see—maybe because of his very puniness—to beyond.

I could relate a similar passion for every type of North American gamebird I have had the privilege to hunt. You simply cannot go to the special places where grouse, partridge, quail, woodcock, pheasant, and dove live and be immune to the beauty of specialized landscape. It is not possible to stir the breast feathers of a lovely bird you might have traveled a thousand miles to hunt and not be moved by the mystery of adaptation, the wonder of evolution.

And if you are open to the experience, many wondrous people, dogs, and events await your discovery.

INDEX